Healing and Suffering

Healing and Suffering
Biblical and Pastoral Reflections

Keith Warrington

PATERNOSTER

Paternoster Press is an imprint of Authentic Media,
9 Holdom Avenue, Bletchley, Milton Keynes, Bucks,
MK1 1QR, UK
and 129 Mobilization Drive, Waynesboro, GA 30830-4575, USA
www.authenticmedia.co.uk/paternoster

British Library Cataloguing in Publication Data

A catalogue record for this book is available from the
British Library

ISBN 1-84227-341-8

Cover design by 4-9-0 ltd
Print management by Adare Carwin
Printed and Bound by J. H. Haynes & Co. Ltd., Sparkford

To my students, who have sharpened my thinking, and my wife, Judy, who has been my supportive partner in my exploration of these issues.

Contents

1. What is the Point of this Book?

I hope that this journey through the Bible will provide a resource for you as you work through issues relating to healing and suffering. My role is not to provide all the answers but to facilitate thinking, to provide an opportunity for exploration and to point the direction to some answers. This journey is to be undertaken in the knowledge that, as believers, we belong to a God who cares for us. At the same time, we are to recognize the presence in our lives of the Spirit who intimately and comprehensively supports us. These are some of the questions we will be examining:

- Jesus was never ill. Should believers ever be ill?
- Is there a method for praying for healing that one should follow?
- Why did Jesus never pray for people to be healed, but Peter and Paul did?
- Is it important that the name of Jesus is used in prayers for healing and, if so, why?
- What, if any, is the association of demons with illness?
- Paul and James assumed that sin sometimes caused sickness. How can one tell when this is the case?

- Is it biblical to 'claim' one's healing?
- How important are the guidelines offered by James (5:13–18) for people who are suffering?
- Why do so many people remain not healed after prayer?
- How often should one pray for healing?
- What is the identity of faith that seems so important to the healing ministry of Jesus and the guidelines of James?
- Can suffering have a positive impact in a believer's life?
- Is it God's will that believers should not suffer in this life?
- What does Paul mean when he writes about gifts of healing?
- Did Jesus provide physical healing for believers when he died on the cross?

Rather than provide an analysis of every issue relating to healing and suffering, I have preferred to try to relate my comments to the New Testament (NT) in the main so that it becomes the major guide in our exploration. I have posed a range of questions and answers relating to healing and suffering associated with distinct sections of the NT. As well as providing a helpful map through the sections of the NT, it also provides an opportunity to offer a discussion of some of the difficult questions relating to sickness, healing and suffering.

One conclusion I put forward is that the guidance offered by Paul and James should be considered first by Christians who are seeking to develop a practical approach to healing. At the same time, the Gospels and the book of Acts, to a large degree, more clearly point us to the healing ministry of Jesus which itself encourages an appreciation of his supreme person and mission. As such, his healings demonstrate his authority to initiate a new era in which people would have the opportunity to develop a relationship with God in a way that was unprecedented.

The questions and answers function as individual components of the book. After reading the introductory sections, it will thus be possible to explore individual questions that are particularly relevant to one's situation or to read each page consecutively. The questions are not intended to be comprehensive. Indeed, the Bible does not provide a comprehensive survey of all the issues relating to the topics concerned. However, it is to be hoped that the most important issues have been explored.

At the same time, the answers are not intended to be exhaustive in their scope. That would defeat the purpose of the book, which is to function as a facilitating source in helping readers come to their own conclusions on the basis of the main facts having been presented to them. It is of significance to remember that where we would like an answer to a question or an explanation of a situation, the Bible is often silent. However, in the silence, we can be confident of the presence of God because he is committed to be with us, whatever our circumstances.

I hope that as we journey through this book together, we will explore and learn about the topics concerned, but more importantly that we will recognize that we are always in the presence of a God who loves us and one in whom we can place our trust. He has prepared us not for this life with its various elements of pain and suffering, but for eternity, where we will share his lifestyle and live in the fullness of the life that he has destined for us.

2. Healing in the Old Testament

- The Jewish nation knew what it was to experience suffering and sickness. In general, the Jews believed that suffering was part of their lot as human beings, but they also believed that God sent sickness to test or chastise them because of personal sin (Gen. 32:32; Ex. 15:26; Lev. 26:14–16). Thus, those who were ill were often deemed to be impure (Lev. 13:1–59) and a stigma was associated with them (Ps. 38:11; Jn. 9:2). Because of the deep-seated belief that God sent sickness (Deut. 32:39), the Jews were often uncertain as to whether they should seek the help of a doctor. The Old Testament (OT) indicates that physicians were valuable[1] and healing remedies were not condemned,

[1] Ex. 21:19; Is. 1:6, 38:21; Jer. 8:22; b. *Ber.* 60a (which asserts that the healing skill of the physician is granted by God); *Ant.* 1.208; 6.166, 168; 8.45; 10.25 … in the latter, Josephus adds information to the OT records concerning the involvement of physicians and the exorcistic skills of Solomon (*Ant.* 8.2) Ben Sira 38:1–15 provides a unique and positive insight into the role of the physician. However, the Mishnah (*Kidd.* 82a; also Philo, *De Sac. Abel. Et Cai.*, 69–71) records a negative opinion, identifying the best of doctors as destined for Gehenna.

though healings were normally achieved by prophets rather than healers, physicians being infrequently recorded in Jewish literature (in general, priests legislated concerning issues of purity and did not provide therapy).

- However, although healings sometimes occurred at the hands of prophets, notably Elijah (1 Kgs. 17:17–24) and Elisha (2 Kgs. 4:8–37), the basic maxim, as located in Exodus 15:26, was 'I am the Lord, your healer' (Ps. 103:3). Healing was often associated with prayer (Gen. 20:7,17) and anyone who was healed of an illness was deemed to be very fortunate and encouraged to thank God. The provision of health, including fertility and long life (Deut. 7:12–14), was recognized as a gift of God and a blessing granted to obedient Jews.

- Protection from sickness was available and wisdom was understood to be an antidote (Prov. 3:7,8, 4:20–22), as were positive character attitudes (Prov. 14:30, 15:13).

- There is evidence that some Jews realized that personal sin was not always the cause of sickness. The book of Job provides the clearest example of a righteous man (Job 2:3) who was nevertheless ill, the book being an exploration of the fact that suffering need not be the result of one's own sin but due to other factors. Although Job's sickness was sanctioned by God (2:4–7), it was not to chastise or discipline him. Similarly, Elisha is described as being ill towards the end of his life (2 Kgs. 13:14), though he still functioned as a prophet and there is no indication that personal sin may have caused the sickness.

- However, for the majority of Jews, the association of personal sin with sickness was a deep-seated conviction and one that Jesus would have to overcome in his ministry.

Have the Promises of the OT Concerning Healing and Sickness been Transferred to Christians Today?

Exodus 15:26 and Deuteronomy 7:12–15 promised protection from sickness to the Jews if they kept God's commandments. The question to be answered relates to whether the promise of protection from healing continues throughout all generations and to all Christians if similar obedience to God's commands is maintained.

In order to arrive at an answer, a number of issues need to be borne in mind:

- It is unhelpful to apply arbitrarily verses originally presented to one audience (in this case, the Jews of the OT era) to a different group unless there is clear evidence that continuity exists between both groups. The promises to the Israelites in Exodus and Deuteronomy were intended for them specifically. To assume that these promises may be transferred to believers today simply because both groups own the same God as their healer is unsafe. Many OT promises, commands and instructions offered to the Israelites are not relevant to Christians. Thus, although God promises to keep the Jews from exile (2 Kgs. 21:8), it is on the basis that they keep the Law given to them by Moses. This promise is of little relevance to Christians, most of whom do not live in Israel and are not in danger of being exiled from their country of origin. Even if the promise was pertinent to Christians, the condition for receiving it is not appropriate, as Christians are not expected to keep all the Mosaic laws given to the Jews.

God offers different promises for various occasions and people depending on their circumstances. Issues relating to the OT Jews are not to be understood as being necessarily relevant for Christians today.

- One cannot pick and choose from God's promises and guidelines. The same chapter that includes the promises concerning healing to the Israelites also contains advice to destroy completely nations in the land (Deut. 7:1,2). Similarly, the exhortation to obey God's commands relates to instructions contained within the Pentateuch, many of which are irrelevant for Christians. Laws concerning food (Lev. 11:7), civil affairs (Ex. 21:27; Deut. 14:28,29), sacrifices (Ex. 29: 10–14) and a variety of others (Lev. 19:19; Deut. 14:21) were prescribed for the Jews, not Christians. The guidance for worship, responsibilities of the priests and elders, the kinds of animals to be sacrificed and how the sacrificial system should be administered – these and many other issues, although part of God's laws for the Jews, are not God's laws for Christians. There is little reason therefore to assume that the OT promise of healing to the Jews, granted on the basis of obedience to these laws, should necessarily relate to Christians, who are not expected to obey those same laws.

- The OT promises concerning healing must be viewed in the context of these facts and not be arbitrarily lifted out and applied to the contemporary church. The guidance offered concerning healing and suffering as recorded in the NT is more appropriate for Christians in so far as the NT is clearly and deliberately written with them in mind. The promise that God heals is actually affirmed in the NT though the suggestion that healing is to be anticipated on the basis of obedience is not. The NT must be the guide for Christians rather than passages that are more clearly intended for the nation of Israel. Thus, although Deuteronomy 29:5 reminds the readers that God had arranged that the clothes and shoes of the Jews should not wear out during their forty years of wandering in the wilderness, few would assume that a similar provision should be expected today for all Christians. That is not to say that God could not function similarly today. However, neither does it mean that he must do so now. Then, it was a divine provision for the Jewish nation, not necessarily a precedent to be set and a provision to be claimed by all Christians thereafter.

- Although a provision of healing in all circumstances is not promised in the NT, that does not mean that the promises to Christians are inferior to those offered to the OT nation of Israel. God's covenant with Christians is new and contains a number of superior promises, not the least being that he will, by the Spirit, initiate a personal relationship with every believer, an experience only dreamt of by the OT Jews. The gift of salvation by faith in Jesus and the continuous presence of the Spirit are but two of the elements of the Christian life that were not available to the OT Jews. Although healing is a possibility for Christians today, even where it is not forthcoming, the supportive presence of the Spirit is a certainty.

3. Healing in the Gospels[1]

Introduction

After studying at Bible college, my wife and I moved to the north of England to commence a new church. Five days into the mission, a young man became a Christian and asked us to pray for his wife, who was dangerously ill. We went to their home and met her. She was in the last days of her life, her young body having been ravaged by cancer. She could barely speak, but was grateful for our presence and our prayers. The reason her husband had asked me to pray for her was because he had read that Jesus had healed people. Three days later, he telephoned me and told me that she had died peacefully in her sleep. Before we finished talking, he had a request. He had read that Jesus had raised people from the dead and asked me if I would go and pray for her so that she also could be resurrected.

---

[1] For a comprehensive exposition of all the healings and exorcisms performed by Jesus in his ministry, see Keith Warrington, *Jesus the Healer: Paradigm or Unique Phenomenon* (Carlisle: Paternoster Press, 2000).

I had spent three years in Bible college, had been brought up in a church that believed that God healed today, but was now confronted with a situation that was beyond me. What was I to do? Was it not true that Jesus had raised people from the dead and had promised his disciples that they would do even greater deeds than he did? Why was I uncertain as to what to do? Surely I should follow Jesus' example. Was God providing an opportunity for a remarkable miracle that was reminiscent of the Apostle Peter's raising of Tabitha from the dead, recorded in Acts 9? The early church was born in a context of extraordinary miracles. Was this to be our experience also? What was I waiting for? Had not Jesus set a precedent for me to follow?

That was to be the catalyst for a lifetime of research and teaching, but mostly learning about healing and increasingly about suffering. I have seen and read of many who have been supernaturally healed but also known more who have remained unhealed after prayer. I have also learned not to be too quick in assuming that all the answers can be provided easily, although I am ready to pray for anyone who is sick.

I am also keenly aware of the danger of providing false hopes, clichéd responses to difficult questions and fuzzy or presumptuous prayers. It is easy to repeat truths that state that Jesus is the same, yesterday, today and forever, but not so easy to explain them when they do not appear to be true to reality. I have often heard claims that the same authority experienced by Jesus is available to believers today but am aware that there are significant differences between the success he enjoyed and that of everyone else who followed him. Even those with clear and remarkable ministries of healings do not experience his success and see only a minority of people healed as a result of their ministry to them.

At the same time, I am certain that the NT encourages the belief that God still heals today. I am also certain that the Bible and the Spirit are available as guides with regard to issues of healing and suffering. Finally, and gratefully, I am acutely aware of the fact that eternity is the context in which all of our lives must be set. Our existence in this world is but a parenthesis in which we stay for a little while, but we have been destined by God for eternity.

In our quest to probe the issues of healing and suffering, our first responsibility is to explore that which the Gospel writers intended us to learn about healing and especially the healings of Jesus.

How did the People in the Time of Jesus Cope with Illness and Suffering?

To understand the healing ministry of Jesus, it is important to appreciate how the people of his era coped with sickness. The issue of health was frequently on the minds of the people of the ancient world, though for the vast majority it was not an area over which they had much control. Not only were the living conditions of many people inadequate, resulting in malnutrition and diseases that resulted from a poor diet, but the health professions were insubstantial, often restricted to only the wealthy, and of uncertain quality. Accidents were common and an assortment of common ailments including toothache, headache, earache and eye disorders that are routinely dealt with by therapists in many Westernized nations were rarely successfully treated then.

More serious conditions often resulted in early death due to the lack of effective medical treatment. Postnatal infant mortality rates were very high, perhaps up to 25 per cent in the first year of life, and life expectancy was not anticipated far beyond 30 years of age. There were also dangers associated with medicine in the ancient Roman world. Attempting to locate a good doctor was a risky procedure; finding one, a rare event. Similarly, the range of pharmaceuticals available and the danger of the surgery practised led to confusion, fear and often major complications and even death. Since medicine was often inadequate, the gods were viewed as an alternative resource.

Most people in the Roman Empire believed in a variety of gods. These gods included the ancient deities who were assumed to live on Mount Olympus and who had previously been worshipped by the people who lived in the earlier Greek Empire. Many people also believed that the emperors were divine and thus had healing powers. The emperor Vespasian, for example, was believed to have restored the sight of a blind man with his spittle. Other gods and goddesses were worshipped in secret cults that celebrated a relationship with the deities. The worshippers were attracted by the possibility of ex-periencing supernatural phenomena, including healing. These so-called Mystery Religions attracted huge numbers of people throughout the Empire and competed for adherents with Christianity. Besides these, it was believed by many that gods and goddesses inhabited the countryside and they were worshipped at countless shrines, requests for their intervention in the lives of the adherents being a normal practice.

One of the most famous gods, renowned as a healing deity in the time of Jesus, was Asklepius. Asklepius was originally a doctor, but after his death people began to attribute to him divine properties that resulted in temples being built to him throughout the Empire, all of them dispensing the hope of healing. People who had needs (physical, financial, emotional) visited the temples, often staying overnight in the hope of their problems being resolved. To be touched by the many harmless snakes that inhabited the temples was felt to be equivalent to being touched by Asklepius, since the snakes were believed to be his earthly representatives. Many people claimed to have received a visit from Asklepius in their dreams and to have received answers to their prayers, including physical healing. The latter often left clay representations of the part of the body that they believed had been healed, and these have been discovered in large numbers throughout Europe.

However, the assumption of most people, even ardent worshippers, was that the gods were not that interested in people. In fact, it was generally believed that they were apathetic to the sufferings and circumstances of people. Consequently, many sought for hope and direction in the philosophies that pervaded the Empire, while others sank into disillusionment and despair. If the gods wouldn't help them, who could?

The Jews faced a different dilemma. There is very little information or expectation concerning the possibility of supernatural healing in Jewish literature outside of the OT. As has previously been explored, the general assumption was that sickness was the result of the sin of the ones suffering, or of their parents. Since God had sanctioned this suffering, often as punishment or discipline, it was assumed that only God could remove it. It was believed that confession of the sin that had caused the sickness could result in its removal, but this so rarely happened that it was acknowledged to be a mystery, to be understood in the age to come. Thus, practically, although the OT expresses the fact that God was understood to be the Jews' healer, hope for healing was increasingly reserved for the future, when Messiah would come.

For centuries before the time of Jesus, the Jews had looked forward to a Messianic era when sickness would be removed. The prospect of suffering being removed prior to that time was an infrequent hope. Rather than experience a reduction or removal of suffering or even an explanation for its presence, the Jews increasingly anticipated an eschatological hope for its removal. This began to be fulfilled in the earthly ministry of Jesus.

What did the Healings of Jesus Demonstrate to the Readers of the Gospels?

In order to work through the evidence relating to healing in the NT, a fundamental issue needs to be explored: why did Jesus heal? There are at least two main purposes for the healings being recorded in the Gospels. The first is to illustrate the person and mission of Jesus, the second to identify important aspects of spirituality for his followers.

Thus, the major reason for the records of the healing ministry of Jesus is to teach the readers about him. The physical restorations, although important to the ones healed, also revealed truth about the healer. The healing narratives are intended to result in the question 'Who is this man?' being asked, closely followed by the more spectacular question, 'Is he God?'

This does not mean that healing people was of little interest to Jesus. Neither should it be assumed that to teach through healing demeans the person who receives the healing. The Gospel writers are clear in their intention of presenting Jesus as a healer who has no peer; his authority is superior to that of anyone else of his time or who had lived before him. However, to conclude that this is all they have to say about Jesus as a result of his healings is to make a fundamental mistake. He is not just a healer, a good healer or even the best healer. He is God incarnate and his healings authenticate him as such. They teach crucially important lessons about him as well as providing restoration for those to whom he ministered.

A number of reasons are focused on by the authors of the Gospels that indicate Jesus' unique significance.

The healings demonstrated his authority

Jesus is presented as having authority to heal sicknesses (Mt. 8:14–16; Lk. 13:32; Jn. 4:46–54), to cast out demons (Mk. 1:23–28) and to raise people from the dead (Lk. 7:11–17; Jn. 11:2–44). The Gospels do not simply describe his power but also his authority, healing whenever, whoever and wherever he wished.

Jesus demonstrated his authority over Jewish Law by healing on the Sabbath (Lk. 14:1–6; Jn. 5:1–6). Jewish Law indicated that the act of healing on the Sabbath was equivalent to work and thus to engage in healing activity would break the commandment concerning keeping the Sabbath holy. But Jesus superseded this Law by regularly healing on the Sabbath, preferring not to delay the healing until the day afterwards. He also touched the sick despite their being ceremonially unclean because of their sickness (Mt. 8:2–4, 9:20–22). Finally, he healed in the Temple and thus demonstrated his authority to heal those who were in the Temple whose presence would have been questioned because of their physical condition (Mt. 21:14). He is presented as having supreme power over all the forces of darkness, illustrated by the way their domination over the lives of people is broken with ease when he confronts them.

taught that God was the one who inflicted
h sickness (Gen. 12:17; Num. 11:33) and the
ealed them (Ex. 15:26). Now, Jesus undertakes
this latter role. The healings of Jesus are presented in
such a way as to make the inquisitive reader consider
whether he could be God. Where no one else could help,
Jesus authoritatively provided restoration.

Furthermore, and in support of the same claim of
authority, Jesus often used his hands in healing people
(Mt. 8:3,15; Mk. 5:41; Lk. 13:13; Jn. 9:6). Rather than view
this as a sign of compassion, it is more likely to relate
again to his authority. Although touch is a Western
symbol for friendship and sympathy, in an ancient
Eastern context, it indicated authority and power. He
who could not be contaminated by sickness, ceremonially or otherwise, touched the sick, whilst at the
same time transmitting wholeness to them. The powerful
hand of God spoken of in the OT (Num. 11:23; Deut. 33:3;
1 Chr. 29:12) is seen to be reflected in the powerful hands
of Jesus.

In the Gospels, Jesus is presented as being awesome in
power. Thus, he is not recorded as praying for the healing
of the sick. Instead, the sickness is removed often with a
word or command (Mt. 8:3; Mk. 5:41; Lk. 13:12). When
Jesus did pray on occasions when healings occurred, it
was not in order to gain power from his Father or to ask
him to achieve the healing; rather, it was for the benefit of
the listeners (Jn. 11:41,42). In this regard, Jesus heals in a
manner different from the guidelines offered by James
5:13–16, where prayer is of central importance in seeking
supernatural restoration.

The authority of Jesus presented in the Gospels
indicates that he was as close to being God as anyone
could be. When people recognized this, it functioned as a
springboard for a step of faith that had the potential of

developing into a lasting relationship with him. It was because of this authority that he was able to achieve his mission, a mission to initiate the Kingdom, reinstating the outcast and forgiving people's sin. However, while many welcomed Jesus' authority over sickness and demons, few realized the potential to develop beyond this. The portrait of Jesus painted by the description of his healings was only appreciated by the minority.

He ministered to the marginalized

As well as the healings providing startling object lessons demonstrating the supreme authority of Jesus over sickness and its taboos, they also proved his authority over people and societal codes of conduct. People who were ill in the time of Jesus often led lonely lives. This was due, in part, to their inability to function as normal members of the community in contrast to their able-bodied colleagues. But, also, it was based on a belief that personal sin had caused the illness, the latter having been sent by God as a form of chastisement or judgement. Social ostracism often resulted, or at least a form of marginalization by others in the community. If God had punished a person, it was difficult for the community to be seen to be undermining that action by accepting the afflicted person back into society as if nothing had happened to him or her.

It is no surprise therefore that the majority of those healed by Jesus were drawn from the poor sectors of society. They included beggars, women, children and those who were, by definition, ceremonially unclean. Such people could not afford the fees relating to medical care. In healing them, Jesus dissolved the social barriers that separated people from each other and introduced them to a God who was not so far from them as they may have feared.

Matthew records Jesus' healing ministry as being directed to people on the margins of society (8:1–13, 9: 27–30, 15:22), as does Mark, who includes the healing of non-Jews (7:31–37) and the ritually impure (5:25–34). Similarly, Luke (4:16–30) records the sermon preached in Nazareth in which Jesus declares that he had come to minister to those on the perimeter of society, this theme permeating the Gospel, Jesus being presented as healing Gentiles (7:1–10, 17:11–19) and those excluded from society (8:26–39).

The significance of this is not simply to illustrate that Jesus had compassion on those rejected by society so much as to demonstrate his authority to incorporate them back into society as fully contributing members. This reintegration was coupled with the new revelation that God had not rejected them, the evidence for this being that their illness had been removed. Since God was reckoned to be the only one capable of this trans-formation, it was assumed that he must have caused it. In this regard, Jesus is presented as fulfilling the prophecies concerning a new age in which God's mercy would be fully revealed (Is. 49:13; Ezek. 39:25). God, in the person of Jesus, had come to touch hurt humanity and infuse his wholeness into lives that had been broken and scarred.

The healing of lepers provides an example of this authority to reintegrate those who had been excluded by society. Indeed, the first specific healing of an individual, as recorded by Matthew, is of a leper (8:1–4). What is of particular significance is the seriousness with which the disease was treated in Jewish society of the time. Because of its link with uncleanness and divine judgement, leprosy resulted in the exclusion of the sufferer from the community and sacred sites (Lev. 13:9,45,46). At the same time, it was God alone who was viewed as the one who could heal the disease. Jesus is presented as the one who heals the leper; he does that which only God can do.

Each Gospel writer, in telling the story, records that Jesus stretched out his hand and touched the leper. Although Moses (Num. 12:10–15) and Elisha (2 Kgs. 5: 1–14) were involved in the healing of lepers, they did not touch them in the process. This is not an incidental detail. By touching the untouchable, Jesus broke the Jewish Law and also risked ceremonial uncleanness (Lev. 5:3). Rather than view this as a deliberate act of presumption or provocation designed to undermine the sanctity or importance of the Law, it is preferable to understand this as the commencement of a process of reintegration for the victim, a journey back into society, to be formally completed by his visit to the priests as prescribed by the Law.

Leprosy ceremonially contaminated those who came into contact with it; Jesus is shown to be above the legalism that marginalized people and immune to ceremonial contamination. By reaching out to touch and heal this marginalized man, Jesus made possible the leper's reintegration into society. Jesus transformed the life of an outcast by cleansing him, and the message to the leaders of official religion was clear: Jesus is the one who determines the entrance and the boundaries of the Kingdom, not they. Jesus was determined to break the barriers caused by sickness that resulted in the isolation of those afflicted. He lived among the powerless and poor, touching and transforming them without himself being tainted. As such, he is presented as the facilitator of this transferral from a living death to a fulfilled life.

Thus, the healings of Jesus are provided as records of Jesus meeting the marginalized and dispossessed, providing hope for the hopeless and help for the helpless. Through his healings, he offered freedom to those bound by illness or demonic influence, and any attendant societal or religious restrictions. He made it possible for them to be reintegrated into society and into their faith community whilst also enabling them to be productive again. Although not all benefited fully from the potential provided by Jesus to actualize their freedom, his healing ministry encapsulated his integrative mission to humanity in its weakness. This determination to minister to the marginalized must be more frequently reflected in contemporary Christian healing.

He initiated the Kingdom

The healings and exorcisms of Jesus also functioned as demonstrations that a new Kingdom had been established (Mt. 4:23,24, 9:35, 12:22–29; Lk. 9:1,2). This new era was prophesied as being one in which the Messiah would make it possible for his followers to relate to God in a more intimate way than had been previously been possible. Although there is limited direct evidence in Jewish literature that the Messiah was expected to effect miracles, it was anticipated in later Judaism and in popular thought that the Kingdom of God would be introduced by healings achieved by the Messiah. Jesus, by his healings, was presented by the Gospel writers as the Messiah.

In healing people, Jesus revealed something of life as God intended it, unburdened by physical weakness. Although this is never completely demonstrated in our earthly lives, Jesus' healings anticipated the life to come after death. In this respect, every healing of Jesus reflected the final victory over death and authenticated his message of the arrival of a new Kingdom. The healings functioned as parables, demonstrating that a new Kingdom had been initiated by none other than

Jesus the Messiah, in fulfillment of prophecy. However, the writers intended that the readers should recognize that Jesus was more significant than the Messiah. They presented him as the King of the Kingdom through whom comprehensive salvation was available, of which physical healing was only a part.

He fulfilled prophecy

In order for Jesus to be accepted as Messiah, it was important that he be seen to have fulfilled OT prophecies concerning the Messiah. Consequently, in his healing ministry, Jesus is often presented as the fulfilment of OT prophecy (Mt. 12:15–21; Lk. 4:18–21). Thus, Matthew 8:16,17 records a large number of people being healed by Jesus, an occurrence which the author interprets as being the fulfilment of Isaiah 53:4, a passage which relates to the Messiah. Similarly, in Matthew 11:4–6, Jesus responds to a question from John the Baptist concerning his identity by pointing to his healing and preaching ministry as evidence of his status and mission. Jesus encouraged John's faith in him and his ministry by showing how his healing and preaching fulfilled the popular expectations of the Messiah.

He forgave sins

Despite all that the healings demonstrated of the authority of Jesus, the Gospel writers realized that there was something more important at stake in their presentation of Jesus. There were other healers in the time of Jesus, though none were so successful as he. But there was no one who claimed, with any degree of authenticity, to be able to forgive sins. The Gospel writers emphasized this aspect of Jesus' ministry, proving it by telling stories of his ability to heal the sick.

This was because the Jews assumed a connection between sickness and sin, often stated in the OT (Ex. 32:35; Lev. 10:1,2; Num. 11:1). Thus, for the Jews, if someone was ill, it indicated that he or she must have sinned. Thus, when Jesus healed people who were ill, he simultaneously proved his authority to forgive sins. In dealing with their sicknesses, he demonstrated that, according to their beliefs, he must also have dealt with the underlying sin that must have caused the sickness. At the same time, when the Gospel writers described Jesus as having the authority to forgive sins, they did so knowing that this was a prerogative belonging exclusively to God.

Jesus presented a new era in which he offered release from bondage, both physical and spiritual. In healing people, he was also seen to be dealing with the apparent cause of that illness, even when no repentance had been offered. He proved his authority to deal with sin when he dealt with illness. The healing recorded in Matthew 9:1–8 provides the author with an opportunity to authenticate this authority of Jesus to forgive sins even though the individual concerned did not even request forgiveness. Nevertheless, Matthew illustrates the importance of forgiveness in the mission of Jesus by making it central to the story, the healing viewed almost as a bonus.

It is significant to note that Jesus never suggested that a person should confess any sins before they qualified for physical healing. He never unambiguously associated personal sin with the cause of a person's sickness. This does not mean that there is never a relationship between sin and sickness. However, to people who assumed an integral link between sin and sickness, it illustrated the authority of Jesus, for he could illustrate his authority to forgive sin by providing healing. This sovereign amnesty demonstrated the uniqueness of Jesus and his ministry.

He did that which only God could do. At the same time, the absence on his part actually to associate sickness with sin acted as a healthy corrective to the Jewish assumption that personal sin was always the cause of sickness.

Jesus announced the good news that sickness was not necessarily the result of personal sin. In healing people, he allowed them to be welcomed back into the community because he removed their illnesses, assumed to be God's mark against them. At the same time, this revealed something to them about Jesus. They knew that the only one who had authority to heal was God. If Jesus healed everyone who came to him for healing, it indicated, at the very least, that he must be functioning with God's approval. However, to those who were perceptive, the healings of Jesus provided them with the opportunity to recognize that he was more than simply a prophet doing the will of God. Instead, they began to consider the impossible – he was God in the body of a human being.

He provided opportunities for people to believe in him

A major reason for the healings and exorcisms of Jesus was to provide opportunities for people to consider his identity (Mt. 9:1–8,32–34; Lk. 13:10–17, 17:11–19; Jn. 4:46–54, 5:2–47). In this regard, they functioned as important catalysts for acceptance or rejection, providing people with the opportunity to trust Jesus and recognize him as being more than a healer. The miracles of Jesus did not always lead to discipleship. Sometimes they led to opposition, while on other occasions they resulted in praise being offered to God. However, they always functioned as evidence that a new Kingdom was present and that demanded a response.

For John, in particular, the healings were identified as 'signs', each providing the readers with a springboard to accept Jesus as the Son of God. John 10:38 and 14:11 reveal that one of their purposes was to provide an opportunity for an accurate perception of Jesus while 20:31 states that they were recorded to enable the readers to know that he was the Christ, the Son of God. They functioned as signposts to a more developed appreciation of who he was. Although, initially, the person concerned may have viewed him only as a healer, the healing provided an opportunity to recognize him also as Saviour. They still do.

Conclusions

- The healings and exorcisms of Jesus reflect his identity and his claims.

- Jesus' healing ministry, as reflected in the Gospels, demonstrated that he was unique. Thus, for example, everyone who came to him for healing was healed. Through it, he initiated and revealed the character of the Kingdom and demonstrated his authority to welcome people back into society. He is shown by the Gospel writers to have authority over the Sabbath by healing on it; he forgave people's sins and proved that he did so by healing them; he showed his authority over the Jewish Law by touching those who were ill and thus ceremonially unclean. In healing them, he proved that he had not become unclean. Finally, he demonstrated his authority over the Temple by welcoming and healing those who, according to the Jewish Law, should not have even been there. His healing ministry demonstrates that he is remarkable.

- He healed all kinds of diseases immediately, cast out many demons and used his authority to achieve the restoration of many. Although similar healings would cause astonishment today, they were sensational then, in an era that lacked the benefits of modern medicine and healthcare. They could not help but encourage people to assume that a new era had come, a Kingdom filled with hope to replace a kingdom permeated with fear. More than that, the one who initiated this Kingdom bore so many of the characteristics that naturally belonged to God that, to the person with insight, it was hard to exclude the possibility that he may even be God. As such, he uniquely offered a route to God that would result in a complete transformation of life and the provision of eternal life.

Implications for the Contemporary Church

• In exploring the healing ministry of Jesus, perhaps the most important lesson is to recognize that the authors of the Gospels described the healings in order that Jesus be exalted in the ways described above. In healing, he demonstrated an authority that belongs to God. The Jews did not even anticipate that Messiah would have these authoritative qualities. Jesus is profiled with divine characteristics, encouraging the readers to ask 'Who is he?' The answer hoped for would lead them to recognize that he was more than a man – instead, he was worthy of their worship.

Because Jesus' ministry of healing and exorcism was unique, it is worthy of ongoing consideration. His love and grace are to be marvelled at; his person and mission are to be the objects of our humble attention, inevitably filling us with wonder that such majesty chose to minister to mere humanity. A study of his restorative ministry leads to a greater perception of the majesty and authority of such a Saviour. He is presented as being as close to God as one can be, with the implicit question 'He must be God, mustn't he?' To Christians who already own him as God, it provides a further opportunity to wonder at the splendour of such a Saviour.

- In so far as Jesus' healings are uniquely linked to his mission to initiate the Kingdom, it is difficult to see how believers today may emulate him; his role was unique and his mission, by definition, is unrepeatable. Healings may be achieved today, but they cannot completely achieve the same purposes as those performed by Jesus. To anticipate the same kind of success as that achieved by Jesus is to place an unnecessary burden on people, especially if it results in the sick believing that a lack of healing is due to some fault on their part. It is necessary to consider the guidelines offered by James (5:13–18) and Paul's discussion of charismatic gifts of healing in order to appreciate better how believers are to function in healing today, rather than to seek to mirror the healing success of Jesus.

- However, lessons may still be learned and incorporated into healing practice today. For example, an awareness of the provision of healing for the marginalized, as demonstrated by Jesus, should encourage believers to provide opportunities for healing not just for believers and in church contexts only but for unbelievers and in non-church contexts also. Similarly, although a ministry of signs and wonders is not the only effective way to evangelize, it is significant to note that the healings and exorcisms of Jesus did function as potential stepping stones to a more developed appreciation of his person and mission. The healing and exorcistic ministry of Jesus provided an opportunity for individuals to respond to God. Physical healing was granted, but spiritual restoration was also made available. In marked contrast to many contemporary Christian healers, Jesus, in his miracles, always intended to take the sufferer beyond the healing, to himself. This aspect of Jesus' healing mission should receive a higher place in evangelism today than it does. Though it should be treated sensitively, the practice of Jesus did result in people coming to faith in him as their Saviour, and the same often happens today.

• It is to be remembered that despite the value of Jesus' healings in revealing characteristics of the Kingdom, the latter is best reflected in the cross. The Kingdom is not reflected on earth in its members enjoying perfect physical health but in demonstrating the life of Christ in all circumstances, whether in health or suffering.

What did the Gospel Writers Record about Faith in the Context of the Healings of Jesus?

As well as expressing qualities and aspects of the mission and person of Jesus, his healings often provided opportunities for Jesus to teach his followers concerning discipleship. The Gospel writers sought to transmit these lessons faithfully for the benefit of their readers. Lessons about the importance of obedience (Mt. 7:21–23; Mk. 2:40–45), humility (Mk. 9:38–41), serving one another (Mt. 8:14,15) and the necessity of developing an ongoing relationship with Jesus are presented in the context of healings. However, the main lesson for followers of Jesus relates to the topic of faith.

The concept of 'faith' is significant in each of the Gospels in the context of Jesus' healings; its meaning is therefore of vital importance. An examination of the use of this term in the Gospels is an important element in this process of identifying what it actually means.

What is faith?

The basic meaning of the word 'faith' in the OT is that of 'trust' and/or 'trustworthiness'. Similarly, in the NT, it is correctly translated as 'trust' or 'a readiness to believe' (Mt. 8:10, 9:2; 1 Pet. 1:21). In the healing narratives recorded in the Gospels, the word 'faith' is used to define trust both in the person and mission of Jesus and also in his willingness and ability to provide healing (Mt. 8:13, 9:22,28,29, 15:28). It is contrasted with doubt and uncertainty (Mt. 17:20, 21:21,22).

What is to be determined is how this trust is to be understood with regard to the healing ministry of Jesus. A number of questions may be posed. Did Jesus only heal people when enough faith had been demonstrated? Did he only heal in response to faith being expressed by one who had asked for help? What was it that he was commending when he marvelled at the faith of some of those who came to him for help? How does this relate to healing today?

What is the identity of the faith referred to in the Gospels?

The faith expressed in the Gospels by those who came to Jesus for healing may best be understood as a belief on their part that Jesus could help them. For the centurion, it was demonstrated by his belief that Jesus could heal without touching the one who was ill (Mt. 8:5–13). For the Canaanite woman who sought the help of Jesus to exorcize her daughter of a demon, it was demonstrated by her readiness to believe that he had come to help Gentiles as well as Jews (Mt. 15:22–28). For the woman with the haemorrhage, it was demonstrated by her readiness to touch the hem of Jesus' cloak, believing that he had sufficient power to deal with her condition (Mt. 9:20–22). For the friends of the paralyzed man, it was demonstrated by their bringing their friend to Jesus in the first place (Mt. 9:1–2). For the blind men, it was evidenced by their asking Jesus to help them, when others suggested that they should be quiet (Mt. 20:29–33).

For each of these, and others, there is one fundamental element: they recognized that Jesus could help them. It is that simple and yet that profound. Despite their limited knowledge of Jesus, they nevertheless believed that he was different. There was something about him that encouraged them to come to him for help, and when they did, he never disappointed them, for everyone who came to him for healing was healed.

Sometimes, their faith appears to be weak, but it is always sufficient for Jesus. Thus, even though the father of the demonized child asks Jesus to help his unbelief (Mk. 9:24), there is no mention of Jesus acceding to his request. It is possible that the man feared that his level of trust that Jesus could expel the demon was insufficient for Jesus to perform the exorcism, but in reality, he had expressed all the faith that was needed by coming to Jesus in the first place and asking for his help.

The faith that Jesus commended involved a willing-ness to trust him. This is a progression from the OT era, when that which was needed for health and healing was obedience to God (Ex. 23:24–26). In the Gospels, a dif-ferent quality of faith is anticipated, faith that recognizes that Jesus could do that which was requested.

Was faith mentioned in the Gospel stories as an important feature of every healing?

Although faith is often mentioned in the context of the healings of Jesus, there are occasions when it is not mentioned (Lk. 13:10–17, 14:1–6) and other occasions when Jesus healed without even being asked to do so (Lk. 22:50,51).

Nobody expected Jesus to raise Lazarus from the dead before he did so (Jn. 11:5–44). Neither the man who had been paralyzed for thirty-eight years (Jn. 5:1–15) nor the man blind from birth (Jn. 9:1–41) had any knowledge of the identity of Jesus before they were healed, neither is there any request that he heal them. Nevertheless, in demonstration of his authority, Jesus healed them. He did not need people to express faith before he healed them. Some asked him and were healed; others didn't and were still healed. But those who recognized his authority to heal, who, in other words, expressed faith in him, are recorded by the Gospel writers as realizing that he was worthy of their request. This reveals more about the accuracy of their perception than that it suggests that their faith triggered a healing response from Jesus.

Does the reference to faith refer to a belief that Jesus would heal or that he could heal?

There is no indication that Jesus expected that people should have an assurance that they would be healed when they came to him. Neither were they encouraged to claim their healing from him. People came simply because they were aware that he had healed before and assumed that he could do so again. Trust in the capability of Jesus to heal was what pleased him, though he also healed people who did not ask or even expect to be healed.

The faith that looks to Jesus for help is that which he commends. It is the faith that affirms 'he can', not necessarily that 'he will'. This trust in Jesus is not the key that automatically unlocks a power of healing but it reveals the perception that people had of Jesus, resulting in their asking him for help. He did not heal because people had a certain amount of faith or demonstrated sufficient persistency or determination. Rather, because they saw him as someone with authority, they came to him and were healed. They benefited from what he could do for them by simply coming to him.

Some have recently suggested that a person cannot be healed by God unless he or she believes that he will do so. Thus, people have been encouraged to claim their healing, to ignore the symptoms of sickness or to believe that the healing has already occurred. Furthermore, the absence of such 'belief' has been identified as being sin. Similarly, the use of the phrase 'If it be your will' in the context of a prayer of healing has been defined as being harmful, for it sows seeds of doubt that the healing might not be God's will. Finally, it has been suggested that one should thank God for one's healing before it has taken place as evidence of one's 'faith' that the healing will occur. Such expressions of faith are not substantiated by the Gospel data. The faith that brought a response from Jesus was simply identified as a readiness to go to him for help. The fact that, although Jesus healed all those who came to him for healing, not all who are prayed for today receive healing will be addressed later.

Did insufficient faith restrict the healing power of Jesus?

There is no suggestion in the Gospels that a certain amount of faith is needed in order to receive healing. Jesus never sent anyone away with a recommendation that they return with extra faith before they could be healed. In Luke 17:6, in response to the request of the disciples that Jesus increase their faith, the author does not record Jesus saying that he will or indicating that their request was appropriate. Instead, Jesus replies that a minute amount of faith, as small as a mustard seed, is all that is needed to effect miracles. It is the *presence* of faith that is needed, not the amount of faith.

The suggestion that an insufficient amount of faith could restrict Jesus is wrong on two counts. Firstly, the teaching of Jesus concerning faith related to its existence, not its quantity. The person who came to Jesus for help had already expressed faith. Secondly, the belief that a person's faith can be developed to achieve a greater level of success is a distortion of the NT teaching concerning faith. It undermines the majesty, wisdom and love of Jesus, making him a servant of a 'faith' by which he may be coerced or enabled to function. The encouragement by some today that Christians should develop greater faith in order that healing might occur causes heartache for those who remain unhealed. It also reflects a fundamental misunderstanding of the concept of faith as recorded in the Gospels.

On only one occasion is it recorded that Jesus' ministry of healing was partially impeded by a lack of faith on the part of those present. However, here the unbelief on the part of the people is to be understood as an absence of faith, an unwillingness to believe, rather than an insufficient faith that needed more development. It is appropriate to explore this key passage, especially because so many unhelpful comments and practices have been based upon it.

What went wrong at Nazareth?

In trying to understand the identity of faith that preceded healing in the ministry of Jesus, it is important to explore Jesus' rejection at Nazareth (Mt. 13:51–58; Mk. 6:1–6; Lk. 4:16–30). Each Gospel writer refers to Jesus specifically returning to the town where he had grown up and being rejected by the inhabitants, Matthew and Mark noting that it resulted in the occurrence of only a few miracles. After this incident, Matthew records the faith of the five thousand who followed Jesus and were fed miraculously, showing what potential blessing was lost by those whom Jesus had come to teach in their own synagogues.

The unbelief expressed by the people is not to be identified as limited faith in him but as rejection of him. It is not they had too little faith to be healed – they had no faith. Mark describes the inhabitants of Nazareth in a way that is reminiscent of others described earlier (5:17) who rejected Jesus despite having witnessed the extraordinary exorcism of the Gadarene demoniac. They had no desire to accept him or to receive anything from him. On the contrary, they were scandalized by his apparent presumption to speak as he did in their synagogue, resulting in their attempt to kill him. After all, they knew him and concluded that he was no one special. In the light of such rejection, it is clear why they would not receive anything from him – they didn't want anything.

Although, according to Mark 6:2, they were astonished at Jesus' wisdom and supernatural power, they still refused to believe in him. By contrast, Mark records the willingness of the five thousand (6:30,31) and those at Gennesaret (6:53–55) to walk to Jesus, whatever the cost to their prestige or comfort, in order to benefit from him. For Mark, faith in Jesus is identified as movement towards him, while rejection of Jesus, identified as unbelief, results in unfulfilled potential.

Nevertheless, it is to be noted that even in Nazareth, in the presence of unbelief, Jesus did perform some miracles. The paucity of miracles performed does not reflect an inability on the part of Jesus; rather, it reflects the limiting effect of deliberate unbelief with regard to the potential benefits available from Jesus. Their unbelief did not restrict him from giving them healing so much as it restricted them from receiving it. They didn't ask and so they didn't get. They did not want healing and so they did not receive it.

However, whereas Matthew records that Jesus 'did not do many mighty works there', Mark records that 'he could do no mighty work there' except to heal a few sick folk. Some have understood this to imply that Jesus needed an expression of faith on the part of those present to activate his healing power, and that lack of such faith resulted in an inability on his part to minister effectively, though he desired to do so. However, the Gospels do not suggest this and, as has been noted, on occasions, Jesus took the initiative and provided healing despite the absence of a request. Jesus actually needed nothing to activate his power.

That there were only a few healings in Nazareth was not due to an inability on the part of Jesus but a lack of desire on the Nazarenes' part, described as a lack of faith in him. Their perception was that he was a nobody, a son of the village carpenter; why would they ask him for healing when they assumed him to be nobody special? The few who did get healed reveal the missed op-portunity for the majority. Furthermore, if Jesus had healed people in Nazareth, that would have placed them in a state of greater condemnation; it would have accentuated their guilt, not just for rejecting Jesus but for doing so in the context of his providing miracles on their behalf. Jesus' refusal to perform miracles was due to the fact that he realized that such supernatural acts would not result in their acceptance of him. On the contrary, to have provided them would have resulted in the people being in a state of greater jeopardy, for they would have then been guilty of rejecting him despite such clear evidence of his divine authority, status and mission. In that regard, he chose not to heal. To have done so would have been prejudicial to those who were already determined to reject him; it would have enhanced their guilt.

In the first year of my time as a pastor in my first church we held a mission, during which a number of people were dramatically healed. One woman was healed of arthritis that had left her unable to walk more than a few steps without experiencing severe pain. After she had been prayed for, she spoke of a heat coursing through her body and, tentatively, she began to walk. She walked faster, then she ran, and finally she jumped in the air on the platform. I was concerned that she might injure herself, but she was convinced that she had been healed. Some weeks later, I spoke with her, as we had only seen her infrequently in church. Unfortunately, although she had been physically healed, it did not translate into a spiritual wholeness and the start of her journey to God was severely truncated despite such a remarkable transformation in her life. She had received so much but it had meant so little. To receive from God has attendant responsibilities. To fail to appreciate them is costly, more so than people may realize.

Conclusions

- The incident at Nazareth may not be used in a simplistic way to claim that limited faith restricts Jesus. Rather, Jesus is presented as choosing not to heal because of an absence of faith.

- The identity of that unbelief is to be understood as rejection, not doubt; unwillingness to accept him, not uncertainty about him; determination to oppose him, not anxiety as to whether he would heal them or not.

- These accounts affirm the fact that, for Jesus, the healings acted as opportunities for people to demonstrate their willingness to acknowledge his healing authority and, more importantly, all that it represented in relation to his person and mission.

- The faith that is referred to by the Gospel writers is to be identified as a readiness simply to go to Jesus for help.

Implications for the Contemporary Church

- What is of crucial importance is to recognize that the faith of those who were healed in the Gospels was based on the person of Jesus in his mission. To demand such faith of sufferers today, on the basis of which healing is said to be guaranteed, is to misunderstand the uniqueness of Jesus' ministry. There is no record of anyone being refused healing by Jesus when they came to him for help. This further indicates the uniqueness of his mission. To argue that the same holds true today is problematic, for not everyone who has requested healing has been healed. Rather than assume that sufferers may be obstructing Jesus' desire to heal, it is more appropriate to question the premise that suggests Jesus' healing ministry may be replicated in our time. That is not to say that healings do not occur today or to suggest that prayer for the sick is inappropriate. What it does mean is that the healings of Jesus had a specific purpose for the declaration of his message then and the establishing of his mission. His healing ministry sensationally illustrated the revolutionary Gospel he preached.

- Jesus is not to be viewed as the model for modern healing practice. He chose not to leave a methodology and the variety in the healings and how they were achieved indicate this. Sometimes in the Gospels faith is referred to, while on other occasions it is not. Sometimes he used his hands to touch people, while on other occasions they touched him. Sometimes he healed from a distance, at other times he was in the presence of those who were healed. Generally, healings occurred immediately, though on a few occasions they did not. Although one may learn lessons for contemporary healing practice from the ministry of Jesus, not least his sensitivity to people and his distress at the effects of sickness, these were not the reasons for his healing people. Rather, his healings and exorcisms demonstrated his unique mission and his unparalleled person.

- It is often expected of sufferers today to express a belief that they will be healed when they request prayer, the lack of healing apparently being indicative of a lack of faith. This view is promulgated on the basis of a belief that healing is available now as an unconditional promise to all believers, a belief which in turn is based on the premise that Jesus' healing

ministry may be emulated today. Since the Gospel
narratives indicate that Jesus healed all who came to
him for healing, it is declared that the same is
expected today. Too often, this leads to disastrous
results, and pastors and counsellors have to deal with
the consequences. Many sufferers are left with a
jaundiced view of God, who appears to lay heavy
conditions upon them that have to be fulfilled before
healing can occur. A cycle in which pain is followed by
hope, which in turn is followed by disappointment,
often ensues, with the sufferer ending up as the victim
of an apparently arbitrary God and well-meaning, but
misled, believers. Divine healing occurs today and is
to be anticipated in the church, according to 1
Corinthians 12 and James 5. To argue, however, that it
is the guaranteed right of all believers, based on the
ministry of Jesus, misconstrues the unique significance of Jesus' role in his incarnate state.

- Although Jesus initiated the Kingdom, evidenced by
  the miracles of healing and exorcism, he did not heal
  all the sick in Judea or Galilee. This was not due to
  some inadequacy on their part or his. It resulted from
  his functioning in obedience to the will of the Father.
  The same principle holds for the way he deals with
  believers today.

- The faith that Jesus required from his disciples was to
  be equated with a readiness to believe what he had
  already told them about their authority to heal and
  cast out demons (Lk. 9:1,41). Believers today do not
  need to develop greater faith for healing but to
  identify the will of God in a particular situation and
  pray accordingly. It will differ from case to case and
  thus, rather than assume the divine advice is always

the same, it is preferable to listen carefully for the Master healer to know how best to minister. In the absence of such knowledge, it is preferable to pray on the basis of the recognition that God responds to our prayers with love and wisdom, always in the context of his sovereign power.

Significant Questions

Was Jesus ever ill?

There is no evidence that Jesus was ever ill. Though he grew in stature (Lk. 2:52), the Gospel writers do not record whether he suffered any physical weaknesses or sicknesses. There is little reason to suggest that he needed to be ill in order to sympathize or identify with humanity. To follow this line of thinking would result in his having to suffer all forms of illness to be able to sympathize with everyone who has experienced similar aspects of life.

Does God heal today?

The experience of the earliest believers after the earthly existence of Jesus indicates that supernatural healings did not end when he died. Furthermore, countless testimonies have been recorded that establish the contemporary nature of miraculous healings. Although this is an issue that has caused a great deal of discussion, with some Christians preferring to believe that supernatural phenomena, including healings, no longer occur, the issue will not be explored. Other books mentioned in the selected reading provide identify books that analyze this topic.

Why doesn't God heal everybody who asks for healing today?

It is true that everyone who came to Jesus for healing was healed. He did not refuse to heal anyone who requested his help. On some occasions, he even healed people who didn't ask to be restored, like Lazarus, who had been dead for three days (Jn. 11:43,44). On other occasions, he healed people who did not ask for his help and who did not even know who he was, like the invalid by the pool of Bethesda (Jn. 5:6–9). This would seem to indicate that one should expect him to function similarly today. However, clearly this is not the case.

A number of possibilities present themselves:

- *Jesus has less compassion now than he did then.* This suggestion assumes that the major reason he healed when on earth was as a result of his compassion for people. However, that Jesus healed out of compassion is rarely referred to by the Gospel writers. Compassion, though important, was not the prime motivation in the healings of Jesus. Matthew refers to it in only two cases (14:14 and 20:34); Mark, at best, once (1:41, though it is also mentioned in a case of exorcism in 5:19); Luke, once (7:13); and John, never. This is not to suggest that Jesus was not compassionate, but it does indicate that this was not the main reason why he healed people. If it could be shown that compassion was the major motive, or even a significantly important one, it would be appropriate to ask why Jesus did not heal all the sick wherever he went. In John 5:3–5, for example, Jesus chose not to heal all, but only one person, in order to teach an important lesson.

- *Jesus has less power now than he did then.* There is no evidence that this is the case from the rest of the NT.

Indeed, the testimony of the Acts of the Apostles is that the healing power of Jesus was still in evidence then as it has been demonstrated throughout the world since.

- *People now have insufficient faith to receive healing, as contrasted with then.* The issue of faith has already been explored, though it will be returned to again in response to other questions. It has been the cause of much misunderstanding and sorrow; it has resulted in people struggling with guilt and, even worse, believing God to function arbitrarily or unfairly.

The word 'faith' is capable of receiving a number of meanings depending on its context. The faith that Jesus commended is to be understood as a readiness to believe that he could help them. On the basis of this simple declaration of trust in Jesus to restore them, people asked for his help. It is not that he needed this before he could help them, for often he healed even without this acknowledgement on their part. But, when it was present, he often commented on it. The only time when a lack of faith was significant was when it was equated with a readiness to reject him and an unwillingness to believe that he could help.

However, that which must be remembered is that Jesus fundamentally came to earth not to heal, but to initiate the Kingdom or rule of God in the lives of individuals, of which healings and exorcisms were two of the signs. As part of the benefits of the establishment of that Kingdom, healing and wholeness are promised to all believers, to be received in Heaven (Rev. 21:4), and sometimes before.

The faith that is referred to in James 5:15 is best understood as faith received by believers, given by God when it is his will to restore them in the way that has been requested. Here, the concept of faith must refer to something different from a belief that God can heal, since that is self-evident. There is no suggestion that it should be understood to refer to a belief that God will heal. Such a statement may be little more than presumptuous; no guarantee of healing can be assumed on this basis. Rather, the faith referred to, in James 5:15, is that which assures the person concerned that the will of God is being outworked. It occurs when God provides assurance to that effect. Paul describes this as a gift of faith (1 Cor. 12:9), given by God (Rom. 10:17). Little wonder that the writer of Hebrews (11:1) describes this faith as being equivalent to certainty.

• The final option is that *it is possible that some people are not healed today when a request for healing is made for a reason that may not be revealed until the next life begins.* Such a response would not be because he does not care for the sufferer, that the sufferer does not deserve to be healed or that Jesus' power is limited. Such a decision on his part must be acknowledged in the context of eternity in which our present sufferings and lives are but short moments.

As a pastor, lecturer, father and son, I have witnessed many people who have experienced many forms of illness. I have prayed for many and have seen many restored to full physical health, but have also known of many who have remained ill or even died, some very young, others in pain. I have sat with couples whose children have died and supported them through the dark hours of anxiety, counselled them when they had experienced disappointment resulting from listening to some who had presumed that God had told them that the child would be healed, only to see that presumption fail. I have learned to trust in God who knows best and to seek to enable those who have a suffering relative or friend to do the same. That is not always an easy route, nor is it one that removes the issues of pain and fear, but it is better than promising restoration when that is not certain.

One of my students was a young man whose commitment to the Lord was wholehearted and who had been used by God to pray for others and see them being healed. However, when he was a youngster, he had contracted polio, which had resulted in his having to be supported by a walking stick. He knew that God could heal him and that when he went to heaven he would have properly functioning legs. However, he was content to trust in God in the meantime. It did not affect his belief that God healed today, neither did it become a constant concern as to why he had not been healed. He represents many Christians who live in bodies that are imperfect but who recognize that God is bigger than their imperfection and capable of either healing them or supporting them in their condition whilst enabling them to be fully functioning members of the church.

Our role as believers who believe in a God who provides wholeness is to walk with those who suffer and with their friends and families during that experience. We are to be the ones who stand with them and on their behalf before the Lord, asking that his resources be made available to them. Our responsibility is to remain with them as part of our commitment to them, not to offer quick recipes for restoration or texts that seem to promise healing for all but in reality do not. If we do the latter, we are in danger of being like Job's comforters, his so-called friends, who thought they knew the mind of God before taking time to listen to God and to Job.

Chris was a young Christian who had suffered for much of his life with severe migraines. They occurred for a variety of reasons, it seemed, but the consequence of each one was that he had to go to a darkened room and lie in silence and wait for the attack to subside. He had prayed many times for healing and although, on occasions, the migraines did reduce quickly, the fundamental problem remained. That which made it more bearable was that often, in the process of recovering from some of the attacks, he spoke of experiencing the presence of God as a warm blanket that left him feeling encouraged. For Chris, it was God's way of revealing that he was with him. We don't know why God has not removed the problem, but we do know that God is not removed from Chris.

It is wise to acknowledge that healing does not always occur after prayer and that this is not necessarily due to some inadequacy on the part of the one(s) praying or those who are receiving prayer. Suffering is part of life; it does not sidestep the Christian. It is part of the package of life in a world that has been harmed by sin. However, in all our contexts of suffering, God has committed himself to be present with us. This means that his supportive resources are available and directed to us whenever we are suffering.

Jesus demonstrated that he had authority over all painful aspects of life, including sickness, though it is clear that he did not remove all of it. Instead, he provided the Spirit to be the one who functions as our heavenly supporter but on earth, with us. Jesus shocked his disciples by informing them that he was to leave them (Jn. 13:33). In response to their concern, he reminded them that he would return for them and, in the meantime, would be preparing a home for them (Jn. 14:1–3). However, he also stated that the Spirit would be their counsellor and support in his absence (Jn. 14:16). He would provide all they needed to live fruitful lives in whatever circumstances they found themselves (Jn. 15:

1–16). In that regard, the Spirit was promised by Jesus as the one who would lead Christians into truth (Jn. 14:26, 16:13,15) and who would provide streams of life (7:38,39).

With that in mind, whenever we pray for others, we should always remember that we are bringing that person to God who through the Spirit gives us his life. This may involve physical restoration but also, and more importantly, it refers to the quality of life made possible, whatever the situation, by the presence of God who desires to bring wholeness.

Should prayer for physical healing be replaced with a prayer for the wholeness of the person concerned?

We should not be overly concerned as to whether it is appropriate to pray for the healing of others. Unless the Spirit has confirmed that there is an underlying reason for this sickness, be it sin or a lifestyle issue, I always pray that God will bring healing, be it physical or emotional. Of course, we need to be sensitive to the person concerned and to the voice of the Spirit who desires to guide us in our prayers. If a person has been prayed for on a number of occasions with the same request and there has been no physical improvement, it is appropriate to explore whether the Lord may have a different agenda to healing. Rather than remove the sickness, he may wish to enable the person to live with it, and to bear that particular burden with his support, the reasons for that situation being known only to him.

However, if the Spirit does not specifically guide us, we should let our natural compassion and desires for the person to be our guide in our prayer. As part of this, it is good practice to take time with the people concerned, to let them talk about their situation and that which they feel God is saying to them about it, if anything. A period of silence and waiting on God is also important; at the very least, it acts as a reminder that God is a central part of this process and time should be given to listen to his voice and to expect his ministry.

If healing does not occur in a way that reflects our prayer, we should look to explore whether people's perception of themselves needs to be strengthened. It may be that their condition has made them feel marginalized or unable to function as others do in the local church. They may feel that God does not love them or that there is some problem in their life that has caused this sickness and that is obstructing the healing. It is possible that their self-confidence and sense of self-worth have been undermined by the situation. These and other concerns should be addressed and time should be given to helping to resolve them. These issues are often more important than the issue of the sickness itself. The role of Christians is to develop wholeness in each other; it is a responsibility of each member of the church, not just the leaders. As well as looking to the Lord for the possibility of providing physical healing for a person, it is important to provide the possibility of a broader form of healing that encompasses the whole life of the person concerned. In this, we follow the practice of Jesus, who came to make it possible for people to experience his life, a life that reflects the quality of eternity.

A friend of mine has severe physical disabilities. When she was born, her arms and one of her legs had not grown properly. She gained two theological degrees, writing her research papers with her toes. Throughout her time she was a student who was both appreciated and admired by other students and faculty. She knew that God could heal her, but until he did, she was content to trust him. It was not difficult to look beyond her physical condition and see her as a woman of wholeness. There was something authentic about her and her walk with God that drew you to her and to the God she loved and who loved her. One day, she will be physically whole, but now, she radiates a wholeness that comes from a recognition that she is in the hands of a God, her God, who is with her all the time, supporting her and enabling her to be the witness of him that she is. Heaven will provide the location to have all our questions answered. Until that happens, she still radiates the life of God; her body is weak but her personality glows with God.

Our role is to help others feel the wholeness that God provides. Although that may include physical healing, it need not. At the same time, where God does not provide supernatural healing, he does provide the possibility of development of character as a result of which he is manifested to the watching world. Therefore, to pray for the developing wholeness of people is a most important prayer.

It is important that people recognize that their value as individuals is not based on their physical attributes. Thus, a number of healing centres are invoking the skills of the medical profession and counsellors to support people. Along with people who pray for others, they are recognizing that in seeking wholeness for people other categories of the personalities and lives of individuals are to be addressed, as well as physical symptoms. For some, although they may be physically ill, this may not be the area that causes them the most difficulty. A coherent and comprehensive ministry makes healing available to people wherever they are hurting most because it provides the opportunity of targeting their area of greatest need. In doing this, we are following in the footsteps of Jesus.

*Is it ever right to ask the Lord to take a seriously ill believer
to Heaven?*

This is not an easy question to answer, but it is an
important issue to be explored. Otherwise, there is the
possibility that no guidance is ever offered for what is a
frequent event. A number of aspects need to be borne in
mind, especially in relation to the contents of the book
thus far:

- At all times, it is incumbent on those praying for and
  ministering to such people to be sensitive to them and
  the Spirit. To pray thoughtlessly or claim healing may
  be very damaging, especially if it does not occur. The
  assumption by the one receiving the prayer may be
  that the hoped-for restoration may not have occurred
  because of some impediment in him or her. It is
  possible that although one may be led by the Lord to
  pray for healing, prayer may also be offered for other
  aspects pertinent to the situation. Thus, to pray for an
  infusion of God's peace and an increased sense of
  God's presence and comfort are all appropriate.
  Indeed, the prayer offered should be seen in the
  broader context of a supportive framework offered to
  sufferers so that they can benefit practically from the
  corporate group of believers of which they are a part.

- The prospect for all believers is that they will live
  eternally in heaven, which is far better than life on this
  earth. Believers have been created with eternity in
  mind, created, appointed and designed for the quality
  of life that is associated with eternity. Life on this earth
  is but a parenthesis in the context of eternity and God
  has programmed believers for eternity. Death is not
  the invincible enemy of the Christian, though of
  course it is still associated with sadness. Life doesn't

end when eternity begins; to a very significant degree, life begins. Eternity is the time when we will do best that for which we were created: the endless exploration of God. Now, we are like yachts in the harbour, ready to sail on the ocean of God's greatness but becalmed because of our intellectual weakness and sinful tendencies. In eternity, we will be transformed and endlessly discover the infinite clarity and sparkling treasures associated with the depths of God's glory. That is our destiny, not life on this earth in our present bodies.

- Therefore, to ask that the Lord take someone to Heaven, unless it is his will to heal him or her, has a number of potentially positive elements:
  (i) It enables seriously ill believers to prepare themselves for the life to come.
  (ii) It provides them with a different perspective on their current situation.
  (iii) It removes any guilt they might feel for the absence of healing if others have been praying for their restoration.
  (iv) It provides other believers with an opportunity of recognizing death not as the enemy that has stolen a believer but as an opportunity for him or her to be transferred to the heavenly presence of God.

In my first church, a young woman became a Christian and not long afterwards became seriously ill, resulting in her being hospitalized and diagnosed with an incurable illness. As a young church, we prayed for her healing, a course of action that I am sure was appropriate. However, she did not get healed; in fact, she got worse. It eventually occurred to me that it may be God's desire to take her to be with him, even though this went against all

that I had been previously taught. Such a thought
initially seemed inappropriate since, as a young woman,
she had all of her life ahead of her. However, the thought
persisted and after sharing this with my wife and the
leaders, and engaging in further prayer, we decided that
this may well be the guidance of the Lord to help us in
our praying. It was important that I shared this with the
person concerned and, with great sensitivity, I did, whilst
simultaneously seeking to determine what she felt the
Lord had been saying to her. Her response was
immediate and heartfelt. She also had felt that it was the
Lord's desire to take her home but had felt it difficult to
share this in the light of the intensive prayers of the
church on her behalf. Initially, she had actually felt that
she was to blame for the absence of healing because the
church was doing all it could to see her healing become a
reality and yet she had not been healed. She wrongly
assumed that she may have been the blockage. Latterly,
she had become convinced that God's will was different
from that which we had all previously assumed.

Two weeks later, she died. However, we had not lost
the battle; her death did not signal a defeat; we had not
failed her, neither had she failed. On the contrary, she
had gone to be with her Saviour and the funeral was a
celebration of her young life and her commitment to
Christ in the context of severe pain and suffering. We
missed her, and recognized that her suffering was an
alien element in her life, as it is for all of us, but at the
same time, we were grateful that God had guided us in
our service to our young friend so that we could be part
of achieving God's will for her in this life. Her last days
were spent in anticipation of her life to come and in a
devoted commitment to her God. At the same time, her
physical weakness became the context in which the
presence of God was manifested to her and the character

of God was radiated through her to others who met her.

What does the phrase 'healing in the atonement' mean?

The issue of whether Jesus guaranteed healing to all believers before death is often associated with the phrase 'healing in the atonement'. Two main descriptions of this belief may be offered. The one option states that, because of the death of Jesus, healing is available to believers today in the same way that forgiveness of sins can be received. The alternative option is that, because of the death of Jesus, healing is available to believers today, though it may not necessarily be actualized until after death. The former can lead to guilt if the healing is not forthcoming; the latter acknowledges that, in the next life, sickness will be an impossibility. More importantly, it is to be determined if the possibility of supernatural healing relates to or depends on the death of Jesus.

Despite the death of Jesus, Paul (2 Cor. 4:16) notes that our bodies weaken and ultimately all die. However, by contrast, because of the death of Jesus, a spiritual transformation is effected immediately and continuously (2 Cor. 3:18). Although a physical transformation is effected at death for all believers, those promulgating a belief in healing in the atonement generally advocate the possibility of a physical transformation much earlier. Although the latter is a possibility, to argue that it will occur as certainly as the believer will be spiritually transformed at salvation is difficult to substantiate biblically.

The verses used to defend the belief in 'healing in the atonement' may be briefly examined. Matthew 8:14–17 is a key passage in this debate. All three Synoptic Gospels record that during the evening of the day on which Peter's mother-in-law was healed, many who were sick and demonized were brought to Jesus for ministry. However, Matthew also records that the exorcisms and healings fulfilled OT prophecy (Is. 53:4).

Rather than follow the Septuagint (Greek) text of Isaiah 53:4, Matthew instead provides a loose translation of the original Hebrew. The context in Isaiah indicates that the infirmities referred to are of a spiritual kind; in Matthew, physical illnesses are the subject, and he links the prophecy with the healing ministry of Jesus. However, Matthew does not record that Jesus provided for the removal of people's sicknesses as a result of his death on the cross. In fact, the death of Jesus is not in view. Rather, he states that Jesus fulfilled this prophecy throughout his life in his healing activity, as illustrated by the healing of Peter's mother-in-law and the crowds who came to Jesus for healing that evening. Jesus healed people before he died. Indeed, all the recorded healing miracles of Jesus predated his death. Thus, to associate healing of a supernatural nature exclusively with the death of Jesus is invalid. Healing depends on God, not an event in time, however momentous the death of Jesus was.

As far as the reference in Isaiah is concerned, it is inappropriate to view this OT prophecy as the basis for an unconditional promise that all believers should be able to claim healing for all their illnesses before they die. Although Matthew does stress the resources available to Jesus that enabled him to heal in his ministry before he died, to move beyond this and claim healing unconditionally for all is not only poor exegesis and application but also a recipe for trauma, as people are thereby introduced to the notion of an arbitrary God who chooses to heal some and not to heal others, though the reasons are infrequently satisfactorily explained.

1 Peter 2:24 is the other text sometimes referred to in this context. The context of this verse is of impending

persecution and other forms of suffering (5:12); the prevailing theme of the letter is that suffering will happen to believers but that it has benefit in that it stimulates Christian growth (1:6–8, 2:18–22, 3:14–17, 4:12–19, 5:9–10). In 2:22–25, Peter presents Christ as the supreme example of one who suffered unjustly but who bore it honourably. The author also describes the benefit that resulted from the suffering of Christ, the implication being that not only should believers seek to emulate his behaviour (v. 23) but should also recognize that the suffering they experience has potential value, though not to the same degree as that achieved by Christ.

The 'healing' referred to in 1 Peter 2:24 relates to the forgiveness of sins, as stated in the previous verse. The fact that the phrase 'you have been healed' is in the aorist tense indicates that a reference to their salvation is being made as it defines a completed action in the past. It is instructive to note that there is no reference to physical healing in this epistle. It is possible that the author is encouraging the readers to anticipate physical healing to their wounds that have been the consequence of suffering for their faith, but more likely that he is encouraging believers who are suffering unjustly to follow the example of Christ who similarly suffered in his mission.

Thus, the texts referred to offer little basis for the belief that Jesus' death is the occasion when physical healing was first made available; healing was available before the death of Jesus and even before his birth, as evidenced by the healings recorded in the OT. That which is not in dispute is that divine healings occur today. Neither is it in dispute that sickness will not be present in heaven. That which is contested is that Matthew or Peter were seeking to link healing with the death of Jesus in a way that might lead to people assuming that it is as easily available as the forgiveness of sins.

Should healings today be instantaneous, as in the ministry of Jesus?

The evidence from the Gospels is that many people were healed instantaneously (Mk. 1:42, 2:12, 5:29,42, 7:35) and, although not all the healings of Jesus were recorded, it is an argument from silence to assume that some of the unrecorded ones may not have been instantaneous. The few recorded occasions when a person was not healed immediately (Mk. 8:22–26; Lk. 17:11–15; Jn. 9:1–7) do not indicate a long period of restoration. There is no evidence that anyone healed by Jesus needed convalescence, neither is there evidence of gradual healing.

Mark records Jesus healing a blind man (8:22–26), where the healing was not immediate, but partial. This is worth discussing, as is the fact that on this occasion alone Jesus twice lays hands on a sufferer. Jesus healed blindness on other occasions and then it did not necessitate a two-part procedure. There is no reason to believe that the one who could raise people from the dead had difficulties with this particular blindness such that he needed two attempts before he was successful. And so the question remains as to why he did here.

In so far as the author does not expand on the significance of the two-part healing, it is wise to consider the context to gain some understanding from it. Prior to this narrative, Mark records a misunderstanding among the disciples relating to a statement by Jesus. Jesus asked them, 'Having eyes do you not see ... Do you not yet understand?' (8:14–21). Mark described the disciples as having imperfect sight. Later, after the miracle of the healing of the blind man, Mark records another conversation between Jesus and his disciples concerning their understanding of his identity. In response to his question 'Who do men say that I am?' they provide answers; when he asks them for a personal opinion, Peter replies 'You are the Christ.' However, although Peter provides an accurate response, it is soon clear that he, as well as the other disciples, does not understand the implications of Jesus being the Christ (Messiah) (Mk. 9:32, 10:32–38). Although Peter's identification is correct, it was not initiated by him but by God (Mt. 16:17), and the following verses reveal Jesus strongly rebuking him for acting as an instrument of Satan (Mk. 9:33). Peter's perception of Jesus is at best partial; he and the other disciples are, as yet, unable to perceive the true mission of Jesus. They are also partially sighted (Mk. 9:10,32,38).

Mark's record of the gradual healing of the blind man describes a parallel development to that of the under-standing of the disciples, particularly Peter, who will come to a full realization of the person of Jesus only after receiving further ministry from him. As with the blind man, full restoration will occur, but not immediately and not at Caesarea Philippi. In other words, the supremely capable Jesus provides a miracle of healing for one man whilst at the same time he offers a lesson for all disciples concerning their perceptions of his involvement in their lives. The main element of the lesson is that benefiting from the ongoing ministry of Jesus will result in clearer insight. All would-be disciples can take comfort from this: even the Twelve failed to see immediately and fully. The promise to them and to future believers is that their immature understanding will be made complete. Such a message would have been a particular encouragement to suffering Christians in Rome, to whom this Gospel was specifically addressed; the reference to Peter accentuates its value to a Roman audience, given his relationship with that city. If Peter, the Apostle, only understood partially, there is hope for other believers in their misty perceptions concerning Jesus and his involvement in their lives.

To suggest that this gradual healing functions as a model for modern divine healings is not appropriate. However, nowadays, although some are immediately healed in response to prayer, others are restored gradually over a period of time. Although this is in contrast to Jesus' healing ministry, there is little reason to dismiss it as inappropriate or to conclude that it indicates a deficient healing ministry. God functions with unique authority to restore people as and when he wishes. As I was writing this section, a friend of mine visited me in my office. He had just recovered from a serious fall, which had left him with facial injuries, which, he had been told, would need surgery. Because surgery would have resulted in him having to cancel a speaking engagement at a large conference at short notice, he prayed that God would heal him. He sat in my office, his injuries having been healed, the surgery having been unnecessary, the speaking engagement having been successfully undertaken. However, the healing had not occurred immediately after the prayer, though it had happened in such an unusually quick period that he and those who observed it were certain that God had expedited it beyond the curative processes of the body. Others are able to affirm similar occurrences in their own experiences. Rather than this be taken to indicate a deficient form of supernatural healing, it is best to acknowledge our ignorance, but at the same time, where the hand of God is recognized, it is good to thank him. The complete explanation will be available in heaven, but all reflections of life in heaven in our own experiences are worthy of our praise.

It is inappropriate to suggest that gradual healings are the fault of the one in need of healing. Similarly, there is nothing in the Bible to suggest that gradual healings are due to the inadequacy of those ministering to the sick. To suggest that gradual healing is due to the power of God not flowing through the believer as efficiently as it should is odd. It would indicate that the healing is dependent on the one offering prayer rather than God who alone provides the healing. The role of the one praying for someone in need of restoration is to present him or her in prayer to God. It is God who will choose to meet his or her need in the best way possible. He is not restricted from achieving his will by imperfect believers; indeed, to a lesser or greater degree, all believers are imperfect, but God still carries out his desires because he is all-powerful. Ours is the privileged role of partici-pating in the supportive role of presenting a person to God, leaving him to minister appropriately.

At the same time, prayer for healing assumes that, although restoration may or not occur, benefit is to be expected for the sufferer because he or she is presented to God and he always responds in ways that are wise and loving. Given that prayer is offered in the expectancy that a powerful God will in his wisdom respond in love, it is to be anticipated that there should always be a positive result from the presence and provision of God. Although that might not always be physical healing, by coming to God, we may expect that God will come to us and impart something of himself to us.

What was the relationship between sin and sickness in the ministry of Jesus?

A relationship between sin and suffering was assumed in Jewish (Ex. 32:35; Lev. 10:1,2; Num. 11:1–3) and Christian (1 Cor. 11:29,30; Jas. 5:16) communities. It was believed in both groups that to remedy the one could remedy the other, though the linkage differed from case to case.

However, although suffering was allowed by God as an act of chastisement or discipline in order to develop maturity, more natural causes of sickness and suffering were also recognized by the Jews (2 Sam. 4:4; 2 Kgs. 4:18–20). Indeed, the many regulations in Levitical Law concerning hygiene and sanitation show that illness was not always attributed to sin (Lev. 11:1–40; Deut. 23:12,13). Sometimes, godly folk were afflicted with sicknesses that did not result from any unrighteousness on their part (2 Kgs. 13:14; Job 2:1–7).

The Gospel writers record no unambiguous reference to the issue of personal sin being a possible cause of sickness; neither is there a request from Jesus for anyone to repent for sins that may have caused sickness. As previously noted, it was a common assumption amongst the Jews that sickness was often the result of personal sin. Thus, the disciples of Jesus assumed that the reason for a man being born blind must have been either that he or his parents had sinned (Jn. 9:1,2). However, Jesus never clearly indicates that personal sin caused sickness.

On one occasion, Jesus forgave the sins of a paralyzed man who was brought by his friends to be healed (Mt. 9:1–6). Jewish tradition assumed that sickness would not be healed until all one's sins were confessed. Jesus, however, pronounced forgiveness despite the fact that no confession had been recorded. It is possible that the illness had been caused by personal sin, resulting in Jesus forgiving the man's sin. However, it is preferable to recognize that the purpose of this story is to show Jesus deliberately initiating the discussion that is to follow by pronouncing forgiveness of the man's sins. His forgiveness of the man's sins provided a catalyst for a decision to be made by the paralytic regarding Jesus' person and mission. He proved his authority to forgive sins by subsequently healing the man. The man's primary need appeared to be physical healing; Jesus chose to meet his actual primary need, unforgiven sin, and healed him as well. Since the Jews believed sickness was caused by sin, when Jesus healed the man it demonstrated to them that he must therefore have also forgiven the sin that had apparently caused the sickness. He provided them with clear evidence of his authority, but many failed to accept it, despite the proof he offered.

Jesus chose not to link sickness with sin elsewhere and, on occasions, deliberately distanced them from one another. It is not the apparent linkage between sin and sickness that is of importance to Jesus or the Gospel writers, but rather the recognition that Jesus came to deal with both, and that he did so with authority and ease.

One other healing story in which sin is referred to is recorded in John 5:1–15. Jesus healed a man who had been disabled for thirty-eight years, warning him not to sin any more or a worse fate would befall him. Some have suggested that this is a reference to the fact that the disability had been given by God as a punishment for a particular sin and that, if he returned to this sinful practice, he would have received a more grievous punishment than thirty-eight years' paralysis. It is unlikely, however, that Jesus is here identifying a relationship between a specific sin and its consequent sickness. The lack of clarity to this end, the absence of the motifs of forgiveness and repentance, and the fact that sin is only mentioned to the man at a later stage, when its potential connection with illness would be lost on the attendant witnesses of the healing, all strongly suggest that this was not a motivation in the healing of the man. It is also to be remembered that life expectancy for the vast majority of people was little more than thirty years anyway.

Furthermore, the nature of the 'worse fate' is not clarified. Given the extent of the man's suffering for the previous thirty-eight years, it is probable that Jesus had in mind the eternal consequences of a sinful life. Thus, he advised him to aim for a life that sought after God, otherwise, the trauma and frustration of thirty-eight years as an invalid would be inferior to the fate that would befall him in the next life. Jesus provided him with a fresh start and forgave him his previous sins. To fail to take advantage of such forgiveness would inevitably lead to dire results.

What was the significance of Jesus touching people when he healed them?

The use of the hand was frequent in the ministry of Jesus. The use of hands was also a major element in the ministries of the Apostles as they reflected Jesus in their healing activities (Acts 9:41, 28:8). Jesus employed a gesture that not only reflected a willingness to touch the untouchable, but also resonated with the OT image of the infusion of God's power through the hand, indicating an authority to transform without being tainted (Mt. 8:3,15, 9:29, 17:7, 20:34). The fact that Jesus is regularly presented as touching those who were sick indicates a radical departure from normative Jewish practice, for in touching those who were ill, Jesus touched those who were also ceremonially unclean. Religious Jews would have refrained from such a practice. Such an action and the authority vested in it is significant to the Gospel authors and serves to emphasize the authority of Jesus.

Rather than view this aspect of touch by Jesus as primarily a sign of compassion, it is more accurate to identify it as an act of authority. There is OT precedent for the hand being perceived as a personification of the power of God (1 Chr. 29:12). The use of the hand is thus best understood in a healing context in terms of authority, indicating to the ceremonially unclean that while their uncleanness may not be transferred to Jesus, he has the authority to transmit his wholeness to them.

Did Jesus heal everybody? If not, why not?

The evidence of the Gospels is that Jesus healed everybody who came to him for healing, and in great numbers (Mt. 4:23,24, 8:16, 15:29–31, 19:2). There is no record of anyone who requested healing being turned away or asked to return on another occasion. The only occasion where he did not heal people was in his home town of Nazareth, for reasons that have already been explored.

That is not to suggest that Jesus healed everyone who was ill in Israel at the time. There were times when Jesus' priorities were such that he chose to move to other towns in order to preach, although people wanted him to stay so that they could benefit from his ministry (Mk. 1:37, 38). Similarly, although he healed the man at the pool of Bethesda (Jn. 5:1–8), there is no record that any of the others there were healed by him. Similarly, it is to be assumed that the paralyzed man who was placed from birth every day at the Beautiful Gate (Acts 3:2) may have been seen by Jesus whenever he went to the Temple. However, he chose not to heal him.

A number of suggestions may be offered to explain partially why Jesus did not heal everyone:

- The first is that Jesus followed an agenda that his Father had set for him (Jn. 5:17). It is this that determined his activities, not the requests of people.

- There is no suggestion that Jesus lacked authority or power to heal at any time. Neither is there any suggestion that those who came to him for healing lacked faith that itself restricted his ability to heal. On the contrary, he functioned authoritatively and was presented by the Gospel writers as demonstrating this authority in his healing ministry wherever he went, whenever it was appropriate.

- It is to be remembered that, for Jesus, his main ministry was teaching, in particular about entrance into the Kingdom of God, not healing. Thus, Mark presents Jesus' ministry in terms of teaching and casting out demons (1:39). Similarly, Mark (3:14,15) records Jesus authorizing the disciples to preach and cast out demons. That is not to suggest that healing was not important to Jesus' mission, or that of the disciples. However, it was less important than other aspects. Exorcisms were more significant to the mission of Jesus, for while sickness does not preclude entrance into the Kingdom, the presence of demons in a person's life forms a much greater obstacle to being able to respond to the good news of Jesus and necessitates the expulsion of the demons.

- Sometimes Jesus healed in order that a greater gift could be imparted. Thus, although the man at the pool of Bethesda (Jn. 5:1–8) was healed of his paralysis, John records the incident in order to demonstrate that Jesus desired to lead people to faith in him as the Son of God rather than simply as a healer. Similarly, the blind man, whose healing is recorded in John 9:1–38, is described as improving his perception of the person of Jesus, the healing being the catalyst to start the process. Thus, although initially, he knew little about Jesus (9:11,12), he later proclaimed him to be a prophet (v. 17), recognized him as the Son of Man (v. 38), believed in him and finally worshipped him (v. 38).

Although the physical healing was a marvellous miracle, the spiritual healing was even more significant. Although Jesus did not provide everyone with a transformed physical life, he did provide opportunities for people to receive eternal life. In keeping with Jesus' teaching that the Father would never give something negative in response to a request in prayer (Mt. 7:9,10), it is to be noted that the Father always gives something good when he is approached in prayer (Mt. 6:11).

Is healing for the believer promised in the Bible? If so, can it be claimed?

This question has resulted in a considerable diversity of response, with some indicating that healing is the right of every believer, a right to be claimed, while others believe that healing may occur if requested. The answer to the question also relates to whether one believes that Jesus' death results in the gift of physical healing being granted unconditionally for all believers, as well as spiritual salvation.

Some texts would appear to indicate that healing is promised to all believers. However, unless it can be clearly demonstrated that the Bible promises that all sicknesses will be removed prior to one's death, it is presumptuous to insist that this should be a viable expectation of all believers today. To assume a guarantee of healing without textual support is dangerous and can result in unnecessary guilt on the part of those who remain unhealed, or in an impoverished perception of God, who seems to deal arbitrarily with some believers in healing them while others remain unhealed, despite all their attempts to receive healing. Although the Bible encourages the possibility of supernatural healing,

either via charismatic gifts or prayer, it does not unconditionally guarantee healing for believers in their
earthly existence.

Did Jesus delegate his healing power to his followers?

It is significant to note that the Gospels record no specific
healings or exorcisms by the disciples, though they do
record that they achieved them on their evangelistic
missions when sent out by Jesus (Mk. 6:13; Lk. 10:17).
This is probably because Jesus was of central importance
for the Gospel writers, not the disciples. Thus, when each
of the Synoptic writers recorded the inability of the
disciples to heal an epileptic boy (Mt. 17:14–21; Mk. 9:
14–27; Lk. 9:37–43), they identified Jesus as the central
figure in healing. The delegated authority of the disciples
is not explored but the centrality of Jesus is maintained.
Similarly, it is to be noticed that none of the Johannine
miracles is attributed to the disciples. Instead, they are
presented as being witnesses of them, the miracles being
achieved by Jesus.

To extrapolate from the records of the healings of Jesus
that, since he healed, all those who follow him should
also expect to heal overlooks the important place that
healings had in his unique mission. So, for instance, in
Luke 7:22, in response to the question of John the Baptist
concerning the identity of Jesus, the healings of Jesus are
mentioned as demonstrable evidence of his Messianic
status. This, coupled with the presentation of his
ministry in Luke 4:18,19, indicates the uniqueness of his
person and mission.

However, it is also clear that Jesus anticipated a
continuing healing ministry in the church after his
resurrection:

- He delegated his authority over demons and his power to heal diseases to his disciples in his earthly lifetime (Mt. 10:1,8). The description of the ministry of Jesus to the sick in Matthew 9:35 is identical to that which the disciples are also commissioned to do for the sick, as recorded in Matthew 10:1. The implication is that they are to do as their Master had done.

- Matthew recorded Jesus as commissioning the disciples to a ministry of healing in the context of preaching the Kingdom, though only to Jews (Mt. 10:6,7). Mark specified that they were sent out to preach and cast out demons, achieving both as well as healing the sick (Mk. 6:7,13). Luke recorded that they were sent out to preach the Kingdom and to heal (Lk. 9:2). Each author thus places the healing activities in a framework of preaching, and Matthew and Luke specifically relate that preaching to the Kingdom.

- It is not to be assumed that this commission, given to the Twelve, is necessarily also meant to be undertaken by the larger church. Indeed, the commission in Matthew 10:8 and parallel texts is located in the context of a number of instructions for evangelism that had relevance only for the Twelve, though principles may be drawn from it to apply to other contexts and eras. However, if this commission was meant to set the standard for ministry today, there is a marked lack of resurrections occurring. Similarly, other injunctions of Jesus are (rightly) ignored by believers today, including his instruction to go only to 'the lost sheep of the house of Israel'. The commissions of Jesus to the disciples were specifically for his disciples. However, other texts indicate that healings may occur through the ministry of believers

(1 Cor. 12:9,30; Jas. 5:14–18) and it is valid to believe
that healings and exorcisms are part of the mission of
the church today.

- The commissioning of the Seventy (Lk. 10:1,8,9,17) is
  similar to the commissioning of the Twelve, though
  the debriefing of the former suggests a more closely
  circumscribed ministry. It appears that the Seventy
  were limited to a particular commission, for they are
  not mentioned again.

- Most importantly, Jesus' final commission to the
  eleven disciples (Mt. 28:19,20 [not including Mk.
  16:17, which is contained in the disputed longer
  ending of Mark]) does not refer specifically to either
  healing or exorcism. Authority is mentioned only in
  the context of Jesus' statement that all authority
  belongs to him (Mt. 28:18): Jesus maintains the central
  position. The final words of Jesus to the disciples, as
  recorded by Matthew and Luke (24:49), include
  references to preaching but not to healing.
  Nevertheless, it is not to be assumed that healing is
  therefore an inappropriate element in the future
  mission of the disciples. Mark records Jesus
  commissioning his disciples to preach and cast out
  demons (6:7) but they also healed the sick (6:13). It is
  probable that such supernatural activity is to be
  assumed in the commission recorded in Matthew
  28:19,20. However, it is instructive to note its absence
  if only to recognize the priority of preaching and the
  making of disciples.

- Mark 16:17–20 records that miraculous signs will
  accompany those who believe. It is anticipated that
  they will heal the sick as a result of the laying on of
  hands. This activity was recognized as having value
  in confirming the message they preached. It is

important to evaluate the authenticity of these verses before discussing the significance of their content; such evaluations have been carried out in depth elsewhere. The fact that miracles confirmed the preaching of the gospel, and occurred at the hands of believers, is recorded in the book of Acts (2:43, 6:7,8, 9:36–42, 14:3). Other actions recorded in Mark 16: 17–20 are referred to in later NT books. Thus, Acts records an exorcism being carried out that incorporated the name of Jesus in the procedure (16:16–18), an instance of supernatural protection from serpents (28:3–6) and occasions of laying on of hands in order to perform healings (9:17, 20:10, 28:8). Therefore, although there is uncertainty regarding the authorship of the longer ending of Mark, the recorded promises are identified as being fulfilled later. Nevertheless, this commission is also to the Twelve; it is uncertain as to whether it should be assumed that it may be automatically appropriated by later believers.

A number of reasons may be thus provided for questioning the assumption that the authority Jesus delegated to the Twelve and the Seventy has now been passed to all believers. However, these reasons do not undermine a belief in supernatural activity or negate the expectancy that God today can heal the sick and expel demons, for the book of Acts did not see the demise of such events; indeed, Paul (1 Cor. 12:9,30) and James (5:14–18) anticipate the ongoing nature of such features in the church. It is Paul's teaching concerning charismatic gifts of healings and James's presentation of healing in the church that lay down guidelines specifically relevant for contemporary healing. It is to these texts that believers should first turn for advice in relation to healing praxis today.

Since Jesus established the Kingdom of God, of which
healings are a sign, should we not see more healings today?

A number of responses may be offered to this question:

• Throughout the world today, there are many
  examples of supernatural healings occurring, often in
  association with evangelism. Where the Kingdom of
  God is being extended, the principle set by Jesus is
  being retained.

  My wife and I left Bible college and started a church
  in an area that was densely populated, but had little
  Christian witness. As such, it was an ideal place to
  preach the good news of Jesus. Our church was
  surrounded by hundreds of terraced houses, was in
  the vicinity of a prison and was a few hundred metres
  away from an area to which the police preferred to go
  only in groups of two or more. Indeed, the tent in
  which we held our first services was burnt down two
  weeks into the mission. Such a context would benefit
  from a demonstration of the power of God, and
  consequently, we prayed that such would occur.
  During the early weeks of the commencement of the
  church, a number of people became Christians and
  many were healed of physical ailments as a result of
  prayer. Such healings resulted in the story of Jesus
  being broadcast to the surrounding area, encouraging
  others to come and see for themselves. Although not
  all who were healed became Christians, the mani-
  festation of the healing power of God was significant
  in some coming to faith.

  To be aware of the possibility of God healing in
  evangelistic contexts is appropriate. As such, the
  ministry of Jesus and the early Apostles provide
  examples of such an association. The 'power

evangelism' model advocated by John Wimber has precedent in the book of Acts. As a result of people being healed, some came to faith. Therefore, while healing is available to believers, it must be remembered that its fundamental significance in the ministry of Jesus and the early church was in association with the preaching of the Gospel to unbelievers.

- Recent history provides countless examples of the value of healings in the context of evangelism. In an evangelistic mission that took place in South Wales some years ago, a woman and a child who were blind were completely and instantaneously healed after prayer. The news spread until it reached a woman who had been disabled for over thirteen years, the final six of which had resulted in her being paralyzed in both legs and her left arm. During that time, sixteen doctors and other specialists had attended her, the condition being diagnosed as being incurable. She had not been outside her house for over six years until that evening when she went to the church to receive prayer for healing. She was healed immediately. When she returned home, she received dozens of visitors every day for weeks and the message of Jesus permeated the lives of those who came to see her and hear of her remarkable transformation, physically and spiritually. Her fiancé, who was in the Navy, was in Melbourne, Australia, when he heard the news, as a result of which the captain and three other officers came to faith in Jesus. Healing may thus be appreciated as having a potentially significant impact in evangelism.

- It is possible that more healings could take place if they were requested. That is not to suggest that God is not able to heal people without their prior request, but it does reflect the statement by James (4:2): 'You do not have because you do not ask.' Many years ago, a friend told me of a dream he had experienced in which he had gone to heaven and was being shown around by an angel. On opening a door, he was confronted by a room full of presents with his name on them. On asking for an explanation from the angel, he was told, 'These were gifts that you could have received but you didn't ask for them.' Of course, this may have only been a dream, but it mirrors the statement in James. It is possible that Western Christians especially, who have so much, choose not to ask for help from God as much as other believers who have less. This does not restrict God from giving what he plans to give, but it may restrict them from gaining that which could be received.

- It should not be assumed that all healings are positive signs of the presence of the Kingdom. As will be explored later, some sicknesses may be caused by sin that needs to be resolved before any healing may occur (1 Cor. 11:30; Jas. 5:16) and, sometimes, sicknesses are self-imposed due to an unhealthy or immoral lifestyle.

Why did Jesus use spittle when he healed people?

Mark alone, in 7:31–37 (and 8:22–26), includes the use of spittle by Jesus in healing people. To understand this strange miracle, it is important to remember the Jewish setting of the story and the destabilizing nature of the physical condition of the man concerned. The use of spittle was one of a number of actions intended to enable the dumb and deaf man to relax in the presence of Jesus, who was a stranger to him. Thus, Jesus took him aside from the others, probably to put the man at ease instead of letting him be the centre of the crowd's attention. Following this, Jesus put his fingers in his ears, probably to indicate that his hearing would be restored. Then Jesus spat, probably on his fingers, and touched his tongue. It is uncertain if Mark is speaking of Jesus' tongue or that of the man. Again, Jesus was probably revealing to the man that his speech was about to be restored, the image being much more powerful since the spittle had been transferred from Jesus' properly functioning tongue to the disabled tongue of the man.

The use of spittle is unusual, though it is referred to elsewhere in Jewish literature in contexts of healing. Thus, the spittle of the firstborn child was believed to contain healing properties, while that of a fasting man, especially a rabbi, was presumed to possess anti-demonic power. In the OT, the act of spitting often indicated enmity (Is. 50:6). Such an action would be significant in this context because sickness was viewed as an enemy of humankind. There is no reason to believe that Jesus was using a magical technique here or accommodating such a belief on the part of his community, for there is no clear evidence that spittle was used in magical contexts during Greek or early Roman periods.

After the use of the spittle, Jesus looked up to heaven, an act suggestive of prayer, indicating to the deaf man the source of his power. Finally, Jesus sighed, possibly indicating compassion or strong emotion, and said to the man in Aramaic '*Ephphatha*', which Mark translates as 'be opened'. The result is that the man was able to hear and speak clearly. Mark has here given a detailed description of Jesus as the sensitive healer, evidence of which was in the use of the spittle.

*John 14:12 promises that the followers of Jesus will be able to
do greater works than he did. How can this be true?*

Jesus promised that the works he performed would be
achieved to a greater degree by those who believed in
him. That believers are described as being able to achieve
these 'greater works' relates to the fact that Jesus was to
return to the Father. In, and because of, Jesus' absence, all
believers are promised that they can experience the
potential to perform 'greater works', as part of the church
which has the privilege of bringing his mission to
fruition.

Some suggest that the term 'greater' relates to
believers today being able to present the Gospel to
greater numbers of people than Jesus was able to,
suggesting that the Father's work referred to in verse 10
is a description of preaching the gospel. However, the
interpretation of the term 'works' in verse 10 to refer to
the preaching of the gospel is inappropriate. The verse
more clearly relates to the miracles of Jesus, which are
specifically referred to in verse 11 (cf. 9:4). John provides
three statements that help provide clarification:

(i)   The miraculous works of Jesus are valid proofs of
      the unity between Jesus and the Father (v. 11).
(ii) The same quality of works is possible through
      believers (v. 12a).
(iii) Even greater works are possible to believers because
      Jesus was going to the Father (v. 12b).

The greatness of these works is not simply in their
numbers or spectacular nature. To suggest that believers
will be able to achieve greater works than Jesus in terms
of greater dramatic impact, caused by scenarios that are
even more astonishing than the healings or resurrections
of Jesus, is an unlikely interpretation of the text, given the

spectacular nature of Jesus' awesome ministry. Neither is John indicating that greater power is available to subsequent believers than that which was available to Jesus nor that greater power comes through the Spirit than through Jesus. Furthermore, the significance of the promise is not simply that believers will achieve more miracles than did Jesus.

The remarkable nature of the promise is that believers will be able to function with supernatural power despite the earthly absence of the supernatural Jesus. Authoritative power will be granted to believers by the Spirit so that, even when Jesus has ascended, the purposes of God will still be made manifest through ordinary men and women, because they will be living in the age of the Spirit. The references to the Spirit that follow (14:15–27) indicate that it is the presence of the Spirit which is the distinguishing feature in this promise. The perception that a new age is anticipated in which such works will be achieved as a result of the presence and available resources of the Spirit to believers is worth further investigation.

The promise is to be understood as an expression of how the power of the Spirit will be distributed through many believers rather than through the individual Jesus. The key promise in verse 17 is that the Spirit 'will remain in you *all*'. The church is the community of the Spirit, in which he will dwell (Rom. 8:15,16; 1 Cor. 3:16,17) and through whom he will minister with supernatural power (Acts 1:8; 1 Cor. 2:4).

Thus the greatness of the works is best understood in terms of the new context in which they are achieved. The focus is not on greater numbers of miracles or a superior quality of miracles. Rather, a greater ministry is now promised to believers because of the new era of the Spirit.

Although Jesus told his disciples that he was to leave them (13:33), he also informed them that rather than being helpless and powerless without him, the presence of the Spirit would mean the exact opposite. Jesus' ministry of initiating the Kingdom was to be complemented by the ministry of the Spirit through believers. Remarkably, the earthly absence of Jesus was not going to signal a demise in supernatural power. On the contrary, the Spirit was to be their source for similar activity.

Did Jesus leave a methodology for healing that can be followed today?

To study the healings and exorcisms of Jesus as if they were primarily intended to function as resources for practical guidance in healing ministries is to a large degree inappropriate, unless the uniqueness of the ministry of Jesus is first recognized. They are not recorded specifically for believers to emulate them. Neither did Jesus leave a model that could be followed to ensure that healings would always be achieved. Fundamentally, the healing mission of Jesus is to be recognized as a pointer to the supreme person of Jesus; the healing miracles call for an enquiry into the person who achieved them.

That is not to say that healings do not occur today or that one may not learn from Jesus' praxis concerning one's own healing ministry. There are aspects of Jesus' ministry, including his sensitivity and graciousness, that should be incorporated into one's own ministry and lifestyle. However, his healing powers are to be recognized as signposts to him and not necessarily to a more successful healing ministry. He did not establish a methodology that could be learned or replicated in any normative sense.

Sometimes he healed after having commended a person for placing his trust in him (Mt. 8:5–13), while on other occasions such trust was not present (Jn. 11:17–44). Sometimes, in restoring someone, he touched them (Lk. 7:11–17); on other occasions he did not (Mt. 9:2–7). On rare occasions, he used spittle (Mk. 7:31–37) and mud (Jn. 9:1–6). Sometimes the healing occurred after obedience had been demonstrated (Jn. 9:1–7); at other times the healing occurred despite a lack of obedience (Mk. 1:40–45). Sometimes he appeared not to be aware of a person who had been healed by touching him, while on other occasions he healed after engaging in conversation with the one who requested his aid (Mt. 15:21–28). Sometimes he healed the person who asked for healing (Mt. 9:27–31); on other occasions he healed people who were brought by others (Mt. 9:1–8). He healed people who did not asked to be healed (Mt. 12:9–14) and even healed those who did not know who he was (Jn. 5:2–9). Sometimes people who touched him were healed (Mt. 9:20–22) while others were healed from a distance (Mt. 9:18,19,23–26). He cast out demons who brought illness (Mt. 9:32–34) and he cast out other demons with no indication that sicknesses were simultaneously removed from the person concerned (Mt. 8:28–34). He healed in the Temple (Mt. 21:14) but also in the home (Mt. 8:14,15). Although Jesus did not heal in a consistent pattern, in all his healings he demonstrated his authority by ministering wholeness to all.

A marked contrast is to be noted between the healing ministry of Jesus and that of his followers:

- Jesus healed *all* who came to him for healing.
- Jesus never asked God to heal on his behalf.
- Jesus never unambiguously related sickness to the personal sin of the sufferer (contrast Lk. 1:20; Acts

5:1–9, 13:8–12; 1 Cor. 12:30; Jas. 5:15,16 where sin resulted in a physical disability).
- Jesus never indicated that sickness had value to the sufferer concerned (contrast Acts 5:11, 13:12; 2 Cor. 12:7–9; Gal. 4:13).
- Jesus' healings had a pedagogical function; they taught lessons about him.
- The guidelines of James 5:13–18 are markedly different from the ministry of Jesus.

What was the relationship between sickness and the devil/ demons in the healing ministry of Jesus?

Belief in the existence of evil spirits was widespread in the worldviews of Jesus' contemporaries, and both Jews and later Christians recognized exorcism as a valid means of achieving deliverance. There is limited information in the OT that would indicate a developed demonology and scant evidence concerning the practice of exorcism. Evil spirits are referred to as though they operate under the authority of God (1 Sam. 16:14–23; 1 Kgs. 22:17–23), who is presented as being in complete control.

The Synoptic Gospel writers often describe Jesus casting out demons (Mt. 8:16, 8:28–34, 15:21–28; Mk. 9:38–41). On occasions, the demonic presence was associated with sickness (Mt. 9:32–34, 12:22–29, 17:14–21). However, it is not to be assumed that because an illness was associated with demonic activity in the Gospels that such an illness always resulted from demonic activity. Thus, Matthew (12:22–29) records the restoration of a man who was deaf as a result of demonic influence; Mark (7:31–37) records the healing of another deaf man with no suggestion that the deafness was caused by demonic activity. Similarly, while Luke (13:11–16) records the healing of a woman who was bent double for a period of eighteen years as a result of a demonic spirit, other paralyzed people were restored by Jesus with no indication that demons had caused the paralysis (Jn. 5:2–9). Nevertheless, it is clear from the Gospels that, on occasions, Jesus restored people to full physical health by first casting out the demons that had caused the problem. When casting out demons he did not touch the person concerned and the expulsion was often achieved with a word.

It is to be noted that, in contrast to some modern exorcists, Jesus did not expel the demons one at a time or over an extended period of time, nor was the name of the demon incorporated in the expulsion. These are contemporary practices that have little biblical precedent. Neither does Jesus identify human weaknesses or sins in the life of the afflicted as the cause or result of a demonic presence. The biblical teaching is that it is the responsibility of the believer concerned to deal with any sinful habit. The eradication of demons is the responsibility of Jesus, albeit at times through a human channel, as later demonstrated by the Apostle Paul (Acts 16:16–18). It is significant that Jesus did not pray for demons to leave, neither do the Gospel writers record such a suggestion when Jesus first commissioned the disciples.

It is significant to note that John's Gospel does not record any exorcisms. The author chose to use a selection of signs to enforce his teaching and it may be that the exorcisms did not achieve his purposes. The paucity of exorcisms in the book of Acts and the absence of exorcisms in the rest of the NT are also of interest. It may be that exorcisms were more prominent in the ministry of Jesus, given the dynamic nature of his person and his radical message concerning the new Kingdom, and resulted in a violent backlash from his demonic foes. Jesus' exorcisms were clear proof of his authority to initiate the Kingdom and demonstrated his ability to control its development.

The NT does not provide guidance in identifying if a sickness has been caused by a demonic presence. Therefore, such a possibility needs to be considered carefully. A number of suggestions may be offered:

- Before assuming such a scenario, it is wise that mature Christians be consulted, especially where they may have experienced such phenomena before. This is particularly appropriate in non-Western cultures, where demonic activity is encountered more often and dealt with more regularly and quickly. On a number of occasions I have been in Africa and Asia and witnessed people who have been restored from illness after they have renounced some demonic intrusion into their homes and/or lives. The connection between the demonic and illness is much closer in some cultural contexts than in others. It may not be possible to provide a comprehensively satisfactory explanation for this difference, though worldviews may have a part to play in any discussion. Nevertheless, to conclude that it is due to simplistic or naïve thinking or practices on the part of those who are from different cultures from our own is often the result of ignorance or an inability to accept a phenomenon that is outside one's own experience.

    A Malaysian pastor and his wife, who are leaders of a large multi-cultural church and Bible college, told me of a couple who were inexplicably experiencing a series of misfortunes, including illness. The pastor and his wife felt the Spirit identify an expensive object bought whilst on holiday as having a bearing on the problems being experienced by the couple and recommended that it be destroyed. From the moment of its destruction, undertaken in association with prayer, the couple had no recurrence of the catalogue of problems that had previously plagued them. Not all the answers to our many questions may be available. That such a phenomenon is not recorded in the NT is of interest, but it should not remove such a possibility from our thinking. The Bible is not meant to be a record of all demonic activity and sometimes the experiences of those outside our cultures may help us in carefully and cautiously exploring such issues.

- Prayer should be offered for those administering the exorcism, particularly in order to be granted the gift of discernment (1 Cor. 12:10).

- Mature and cautious thought should not be underestimated on such occasions. On occasions, vocal and physical activity develops on the part of an individual and it needs to be borne in mind that, though this may indicate demonic presence, it may also signify physical/emotional conditions. Some years ago, I witnessed a young person exhibiting eccentric behaviour that some viewed as indicative of a demonic presence. However, a mature Christian colleague, used to demonic activity, poured some water over the person to bring her to her senses, for he recognized that she was not demonized but in a state of unhealthy and heightened emotion. The aftermath bore out the wisdom of his action and she received appropriate counselling. To have tried to exorcize a demon from her would have been most damaging. Careful diagnosis is needed in such situations, and asking for help in ascertaining the cause of the symptoms is not a sign of weakness but of wisdom.

- It is to be noted that in the ministry of Jesus few illnesses were related to demonic activity, whilst in the rest of the NT such an association is absent. This may be a helpful framework for exploring the relationship between the demonic activity and sickness today. That is not to dismiss such a possible relationship but to provide a useful perspective.

Why didn't Jesus appear to want to restore the daughter of the Syrophoenician woman (Mt. 15:21–28; Mk. 7:24–30)?

Matthew records this story in the same order as Mark, preceding it with a lengthy discussion between Jesus and the Pharisees concerning that which defiles a person, a discussion in which Jesus stressed the seriousness of internal defilement. The preceding narratives in both Gospels emphasize the importance of placing one's trust in Jesus as a basis for receiving his help and commendation. The most important aspect of this story is not the exorcism of the demon, even though it is the only record of an exorcism performed at a distance, but the conversation between Jesus and the woman, during which Jesus commends her for her trust in him. Against the background of his previous condemnation of the Jewish leaders for being 'blind guides' (Mt. 15:14), despite the fact that Jesus' wisdom and authority had been clearly demonstrated to them, his commendation of the faith of this non-Jewish woman is striking.

Initially, Jesus chose not to grant her request for the expulsion of the demon from her daughter, despite the fact that in previous incidents when people had come to Jesus for help, he had restored them. The Syrophoenician woman demonstrated her faith by coming to him in the first place. At the same time, Jesus gave no indication that her faith needed to be developed or corrected; neither was there any implication that it was deficient. The quality of her faith, her ability to trust him, may have needed to be clarified and commended, but it needed no improvement.

Instead, this incident became a teaching opportunity for Jesus (and the Gospel writers) concerning the quality of the faith that he desired to find in his followers. The woman preceded her request by addressing Jesus as 'O Lord, Son of David', a striking acknowledgement by a Gentile woman, especially when the previous verse has described the Jewish religious leaders as failing to recognize him. She recognized who Jesus was when they did not. She knew that Jesus was able to cast out the demon, for she recognized his superior status.

That Jesus initially ignored her request is unusual, for he had previously ministered on behalf of a Gentile centurion (Mt. 8:7), but Jesus was in control of this situation and knew the end from the beginning. The disciples begged Jesus to send her away, indicating that she had remained in his presence for some time (Mt. 15:23), but he did not accede to their request; in fact, he ignored it. In response to their request, Jesus replied that his mission was to the house of Israel only (Mt. 15:24). His statement had more relevance to the woman than to the disciples and his initial apparent reticence to meet her need was for a purpose. He presented a blunt statement that could have put her off, but at the same time it provided an opportunity for her to respond with great insight. Jesus' refusal to grant the requests, both of the woman and of the disciples, became a springboard for the woman's response. Although the situation did not appear to be promising, Jesus had actually given her the opportunity to reveal the extent of her perception of his identity.

In response to Jesus' statement concerning his mission to the house of Israel, Matthew simply recorded her saying 'Lord, help me.' With this vulnerable request, she placed her trust in him. She came to him on the basis of her belief that he had come to this world, and to her town, to help people, all people in need. She recognized his role to the people of Israel, but she also realized that it was within his mission to minister to others too, even Gentile women. She demonstrated greater perception than that of the disciples regarding the ministry of Jesus. They wished only to send her away, but she realized that Jesus wanted her to stay.

Jesus then created a further opportunity for her to demonstrate the quality of her insight into his character and mission when he suggested that justice precluded his offering her aid. In response to his statement that the bread, which was provided by right for the children, should not be thrown to the dogs, she replied that it would be quite acceptable for dogs to eat the unwanted crumbs that fell to the floor. The woman revealed her knowledge that Jesus' mission to establish justice was also a mission initiated by love. She acknowledged the priority of the Jews to receive the ministry of Jesus, but recognized that her own inferior position also allowed the possibility of ministry on the basis of love and compassion. Although Jesus came to the children of Israel, she realized that those whom they treated as inferior were also welcomed by him to receive from him.

Actually, the use of the term 'dog', in referring to the woman, seems rude on the part of Jesus; it expressed the contemptuous attitude of Jews to Gentiles. If the term was used as a deliberate, provocative description of her race, her remarkable insight into the purpose of his mission is now even more spectacular. She shines as a radiant example of one who, in contrast to the disciples, the Pharisees and the Jews, revealed significant insight into the purposes of Jesus and his mission to cross racial and cultural boundaries to bring the gospel.

The woman's perspective and insight (identified as faith) delighted Jesus. Having provided her with challenging hurdles, she cleared them all with ease. No more obstacles were to be provided by Jesus. The lesson, for the woman, the hearers and future readers, was clear. This woman, a Gentile nobody as far as the Jewish leaders of the first century were concerned, had presented Jesus with a marvellous example of faith in him. She knew that he had power to help her and that his mission precluded any other option. As a result of her faith, Matthew states explicitly and Mark implicitly that her request was granted. The story concludes, the exorcism occurring instantaneously, without any command by Jesus.

The lesson of the miracle has been developed successfully; the exorcism functioned as the conclusion of the story, though the climax had already been established in the remarkable ability of the woman to realize the wider mission of Jesus to provide wholeness for all. This again is another example of a supernatural action by Jesus being used by him and the Gospel writers to teach important lessons concerning Jesus' mission.

Did Jesus leave a methodology for exorcism that can be followed today?

The first detailed exorcism recorded by Matthew and Luke (and the second one by Mark) is worthy of consideration in responding to this question (Mt. 8:28–34; Mk. 5:1–20; Lk. 8:26–39). The common facts, which appear in all the accounts, are that the victim(s) of the demonization met Jesus, the demons confessed their knowledge of Jesus, and were dispatched by Jesus into a herd of swine, which thereafter ran into the sea and drowned, the result being that the people who witnessed the event asked Jesus to leave. A number of lessons may be learned from this story:

- *The authority of Jesus over demons.* Matthew's account is the shortest (seven verses compared to Mark's twenty) and it concentrates on the authority and ease with which Jesus dealt with two fierce demoniacs. One word – 'Go' – by Jesus was enough to effect the expulsion. The conversation, as recorded by Matthew, is also the shortest of the three accounts, being restricted to a question by the demons and a dismissal by Jesus. There is no request that the man share his testimony with others, as Mark and Luke report; the emphasis is on Jesus and his confident supremacy. Rather than presenting a struggle, each Gospel writer describes the demons as being in submission to Jesus while the victim of their malevolence is redeemed. Not only are the demons vanquished, but the quality of the victory achieved by Jesus is such that the man is completely restored.

- *Characteristics of demons.* Each writer records that the demoniac dwelt amongst tombs. According to Jewish belief, tombs were ritually impure places, being closely associated with death and demons. Matthew records that the demons were fierce and malevolent; Mark, that strength and self-abuse were significant characteristics of the demoniac; and Luke, that the demoniac, who used to live in the city, now lived without a home, naked, and under the dominating force of a demon that 'seized him' and drove him into the desert. Such behaviour and attributes were clearly anti-social, degrading and destructive. The self-identification of *Legion* (a Roman term for a group of 4,000 to 6,000 soldiers) is most likely offered by a representative demon speaking on behalf of others, assuming that the truth is being revealed concerning their number. Their frightening malevolence sets the scene for the confrontation with Jesus. What is important in all three accounts is that the power of Jesus is seen to be superior to the most malevolent of demonic foes, despite their superior numbers.

The personality of the afflicted man appears to be indistinguishable from the demonic presence. The personal pronouns in the Marcan and Lucan accounts fluctuate between singular and plural, making an identification impossible, though Matthew prefers to keep to the plural and thus identifies the demons as the initiators of the request to be sent into the swine. It is only after the exorcism is completed that the words of Jesus can be said with certainty to be addressed to the person concerned.

- *The response of demons to Jesus.* Matthew records that the demoniacs met Jesus; Luke states that it was Jesus who first saw the demoniac; Mark describes the demoniac as seeing Jesus at a distance, running to him and falling on his knees before him. Luke too records that the demoniac fell down before Jesus. Whether this obeisance or worship is initiated by the man or by the demon is not clarified. It is difficult to believe that the man himself could have known the status of Jesus; even if he did, there is no reason why he should assume that he was in danger of being tormented by Jesus as reflected in the words spoken to Jesus.

However, the demon did have prior knowledge and was aware of Jesus' superior status and authority. Although this would not necessarily have led to an expression of voluntary worship, it is conceivable that the demon was forced to grant Jesus the acclamation he deserved, but which the demon would have preferred not to acknowledge. The exorcistic confrontation appears to be between Jesus and the demonic force, without the active cooperation of the demoniac(s), who acted only at the instigation of the demon. The confrontation appears to be one-sided and it is the authority of Jesus that is stressed from the outset. Even before the battle-cry is heard, the victory parade is being planned, at least in the mind of the author.

All three writers record, with slight variations, how the demons preceded their confession of Jesus by questioning the significance of his presence in their territory. This phrase used (literally, 'What to us and to you?') is used in the OT (Josh. 22:24; Judg. 11:12; 2 Sam. 16:10) and refers to a declaration of malevolent intent on the part of the demons, somewhat akin to the phrases 'Mind your own business' or 'Why are you interfering in our affairs?' It is probable that there is an implied threat in these words, and possible that the demons are seeking to destabilize Jesus by their forceful antagonism.

The content of the demons' appeal varies slightly between the accounts. Matthew records the demons asking if Jesus had come to torment them before the time, implying a foreknowledge on their part that such torment was to be their destiny; they express surprise, deducing that it is premature. This may be a reference to the Final Judgement. Mark and Luke simply present the demons as asking Jesus not to torment them. Their arrogance has evaporated quickly, for their judge has picked up his gavel. The court is open; judgement is to be delivered and justice to be achieved.

The use of the name of Jesus by the demons is not to be interpreted as indicating their belief in any pseudo-magical properties of the name whereby they might hope to control Jesus, for it is immediately followed by their plea for leniency. Although the concept of power was associated with the use of a name (of a god), it is unlikely that this is the case here. It is probable that the words of the demons are in recognition of the authority of Jesus rather than an attempt to protect themselves from him. The demons cannot help but acknowledge Jesus' identity; their time for bargaining is over and they await their sentence.

- *The exorcism of the demons.* On this occasion, the exorcism is not completed immediately after Jesus' initial command that the demons should leave the man. This is not because it was a particularly resistant demon or that Jesus needed to know the demon's name before he could expel it. Jesus is not engaging in some sort of spiritual warfare which involves a variety of skirmishes before the final battle is won. Although a confrontation is described here, it is not one between equals.

Jesus does not, as a rule, request information about the demon in his other exorcisms, and it is therefore not necessary to see in Jesus' action on this occasion an example of an exorcistic device on his part. The Bible nowhere advocates the usefulness of or need for identifying demons for the purpose of expulsion. Jesus does not need to have extra information before he can effect an exorcism. If that was the case, Jesus would be inferior to the demons who knew *his* identity. It is more likely that the request is made by Jesus to reveal to the observers the intensity of the demonic control. By achieving victory over such a powerful foe, Jesus' authority was most clearly demonstrated. The demons respond truthfully because it is Jesus who asks the question. They have already abdicated their control over the man; they have met their match, for the superior power of Jesus is obvious to them.

The request of the demons to be allowed to enter swine is of interest. Because they are aware that there is no common ground between them and Jesus and that they are doomed, their plea for clemency may be an inevitable reaction on the part of those who have nothing to lose. That they ask to be sent into swine suggests their desire to inhabit bodies, even those of swine, a suitable home for them (Lev. 11:7). Luke alone records the desire of the demons not to be dispatched into the 'abyss', probably, their place of judgement (Rev. 11:7, 17:8, 20:3).

That Jesus acceded to the request of the demons is of interest, though it must not be forgotten that Jesus was still in control. It is probable that Jesus allowed their request to be granted to prove to the demonized man that he had been freed of demons; they had left for good. Earlier attempts to control his problems had failed, but this time they were solved permanently, and the dramatic change in the behaviour of the swine was public proof of that glorious fact.

It is probable that Jesus sent the swine into water to destroy them or at least to end their influence; their habitation of the swine was but a temporary respite. The same demons that made the demoniac abuse himself physically carried on their activity in the pigs. It is the nature of evil to destroy, eventually also itself. It is inconceivable that the demons were allowed to continue their malevolent work after causing the death of the swine and more likely that the message presented by the writers is that the drowning of the swine indicated the demise of the demons. The imagery of water to signify death of demons was common in Jewish thought. Jewish exorcistic practice incorporated a bowl of water into which the demon was to be cast, the moving of the water affording proof that the demon had left the person concerned. This is also reflected in the NT where demons are described as searching in waterless places for a body to inhabit (Mt. 12:43).

To have allowed demons to inhabit other human bodies after the destruction of the swine would have undermined Jesus' superiority and allowed their evil work to continue, despite the exorcism by Jesus. The demons were not sent on holiday into the hogs. They had not had the last laugh; they had received their last rites. Jesus had not come in order to entertain the crowds temporarily but to terminate permanently the demons' rule of terror.

- *Jesus has supreme authority over all evil powers.* Although the incident demonstrates the significant power of the demons, who made two thousand swine uncontrollable, it is the power of Jesus over the demons, and thus over Satan, which is central to the story. Even if the demons attempted to escape into the sea, all three authors have previously presented Jesus' authority over the sea, a point particularly noticeable in the previously recorded story by Luke (8:22–25). It is Jesus who is central to the story, not the exorcism; he is the sensation, not the demons. The message of the exorcism is that Jesus is superior to all malevolent powers, and although he does not look for demons, whenever they present themselves to him, he expels them from the people they are victimizing.

As far as modelling the practice of Jesus is concerned, the following lessons may be learned from the activity of Jesus:

(i)   It is instructive to note that Jesus did not look for demons; they found him.

(ii) It is not appropriate that the demonized person be touched.

(iii) The demonic presence should be commanded to leave in the name of Jesus.

(iv) It is not necessary to shout.

(v)   The demon should be dispatched to Jesus for him to deal with it.

(vi) It is important not to be presumptuous in the presence of evil or to be intimidated by such evil, since Jesus is the King to whom these beings are subject.

(vii) Both Mark and Luke record Jesus instructing the man concerned to testify about the divine nature of his restoration. To testify concerning the centrality of God to the expulsion of the demon reinforces the fact that such divine involvement presupposes ongoing commitment to God by the one delivered from the demonic bondage.

Although not explicitly reflected in the exorcistic ministry of Jesus, it is important to be open to the guidance of the Spirit in any deliverance procedure. There are times when the gift of discernment, as referred to by Paul (1 Cor. 12:10), is an important element. A little while ago, I was to marry a young couple, the fiancé having become a Christian some months earlier. His family members were opposed to the wedding and particularly to his Christian commitment, because of their own religious background. On the evening prior to the wedding, his fiancée rang me to inform me that he appeared to be in something akin to a coma. When I arrived, he was lying down, his eyes shut as if he was sleeping. I sensed that this was a malevolent condition and considered how to proceed. I felt the Spirit indicate that as well as commanding any demonic influence to go, we should sing some songs of worship. After a very short while, the young man's eyes opened and he embraced his fiancée. He had no similar experiences thereafter and they were happily married the following day. The role of the Spirit is an important guide in such situations.

Why couldn't the disciples cast out the demon referred to in Matthew 17:14–21; Mark 9:14–29; Luke 9:37–43?

The failure of the disciples is to be seen in the context of Matthew 10:1; Mark 6:7,13; Luke 9:1,2, where it is recorded that they had been granted authority by Jesus to cast out demons. Their incapacity is to be interpreted in the light of their not appropriating the authority that had been previously delegated to them.

- *The disciples are challenged by Jesus because of their unwillingness to believe in the authority granted to them by him.* Jesus is described as rebuking the disciples for their failure. He did not rebuke the father for he had already demonstrated his faith by asking Jesus for help in the first place. Matthew and Mark note that the disciples privately asked Jesus why they were unable to cast out the demon. Matthew records that it was due to their having little faith, followed by the statement that faith of a size akin to the smallness of a mustard seed has potential to move a mountain (Mt. 21:21,22; Lk. 17:5,6).

- *The identity of faith.* The identity of this faith is not clarified by Matthew. However, by noting that Jesus tells the disciples that their faith was too small, and adding that only a minute amount of faith was actually necessary, Matthew implies that their faith was even less than minute. Indeed, it suggests that their faith was non-existent. This is supported by the fact that each of the authors describes the disciples as being 'faithless'. Their belief in God's power made available to them had deserted them.

Jesus is not suggesting that faith can develop or increase in order to effect a miracle or that a particular quality of faith is needed. Rather, it is the presence of faith that is essential. Jesus is not to be understood as advocating that it is possible to achieve anything one wants, if only one has sufficient faith. Instead, he is pointing to the expansive possibilities available to the one who exercises faith. It is the *presence* of faith that is significant, nothing less and nothing more. The metaphor of the capability of minute faith being able to achieve supernatural effects makes the point forcefully.

One more aspect is integral to the exercise of faith, namely the will of God. This narrative gives no support to the view that it is possible to manipulate God to achieve one's own desires, irrespective of his will. The will of God was fundamental to the life and mission of Jesus, and faith in Jesus can only truly be called that if the will of God is also central to the life of the one who seeks to live by faith. In exercising faith, God's will is paramount, and this understanding motivated Matthew and Mark to surround this story with two statements by Jesus concerning his own allegiance to the will of God, even though it would involve suffering.

The disciples had previously been commissioned by Jesus and granted authority to cast out demons.

Their responsibility was to fulfil this commission.
They had done this in the past and witnessed miracles
(Mk. 6:13; Lk. 9:6, 10:17). However, on this occasion,
they failed to do so. The failure on their part was not
due to inadequate resources but because they did not
take advantage of the resources provided. Their
absence of faith in the resources granted to them by
Jesus created a vacuum as a result of which they chose
not to avail themselves of the opportunity to use
them.

Because of the firmness of the promise by Jesus,
they only needed to obey his words and the exorcism
would have occurred. That they did not is to be
identified as faithlessness. It was not that they had too
little faith but that they placed no faith in the promise
of Jesus.

- *The place of the father in the story.* The father requested
  help from Jesus on the basis of Jesus' mercy, stating 'if
  you can do anything … help us'. Jesus replies with the
  words 'if you can! All things are possible to him who
  believes.' Jesus responded to his implied doubt
  concerning Jesus' ability by repeating the question as
  an exclamation. It is possible to interpret Jesus'
  exclamation 'if you can' as a rebuke, as if he were
  surprised that the man should doubt his ability.
  However, Jesus never rebuked those who came to him
  for help in the context of suffering. By coming to him,
  they were already expressing faith in him. It is more
  likely that Jesus here repeats the words in a positive
  sense, to reveal the potential available to the one who
  trusts in him. Jesus is not rebuking the man or
  correcting his faith. Instead, Jesus is creating an
  opportunity for the man to realize, beforehand, that
  the certainty of restoration is assured because he has
  already expressed a belief in the awesome power of

God, resident in Jesus. The man believed that Jesus was worth approaching, and Jesus now assures him that his faith will be rewarded.

The man's request to Jesus, 'help my unbelief', may have been an evaluation of an apparent inadequacy of his faith. However, Jesus neither confirms this nor encourages him to increase his faith. He simply performs the exorcism. The man's coming has proved his faith in Jesus; his words, however, may reflect a natural concern on his part that he may need to offer a greater certainty in the authority of Jesus. His words are those of a desperate man, representing a transparent reflection of his imperfect trust, but it's enough for Jesus.

- *The relevance of prayer in exorcism.* The failure of the disciples is associated by Jesus with a lack of prayer. Jesus upbraids them not because they did not pray enough, but because they did not pray at all. While Matthew comments on their lack of faith, Mark comments on their lack of prayer; both faith and prayer are integral to the achievement of God's will. Jesus elsewhere presents the importance of persistent prayer, but in this context it is a lack of prayer that is the issue.

  The focus is not on how to achieve power but on the necessity for developing a relationship with the one who is the source of power. It is incorrect to conclude from this story that healings or exorcisms may not occur because insufficient prayer has been offered; Jesus here reprimands the disciples for the absence of prayer. The belief that God will grant what is best for believers or accede to their request only after sufficient appeals have been made to him misrepresents the God of grace and mercy.

Prayer is not a key feature in the exorcisms of Jesus or his followers. It is most likely included here not to articulate the need for a request of God for an exorcism but to describe a lifestyle that reflects a relationship with God and eagerness to determine his will. If the disciples had engaged in this kind of dependent and prayerful relationship with God, they would have followed his leading (as did Jesus) and restored the person concerned. The same relational and prayerful dependency on God is addressed here by Jesus. An ongoing relationship with God incorporates a readiness to obey him and to take advantage of the resources he makes available for occasions that warrant his restorative influence. Such a relationship means that the believer will choose to listen to God and follow his leading rather than be obstructed by the difficulties of the situation.

• *The identification of the demon.* The phrase 'this kind' may refer to this particular type of demon or to demons in general. A hierarchy of demons is not articulated in the Bible, and Jesus nowhere gives an indication that some demons need more prayer for expulsion than others. It is significant that Jesus did not pray for the demon to leave, neither do any of the Gospel writers record such a suggestion when Jesus first commissioned the disciples. It is preferable to regard the words of Jesus as referring to the general practice of exorcism, to emphasize that it demands a quality of life which is to be identified with an ongoing relationship with God, a life of prayerfulness that is associated with dependency on God rather than specific prayers to be offered when exorcisms are being undertaken.

Implications for the Contemporary Church

- The healing narratives are to be viewed as important vehicles presenting, in particular, invaluable lessons for the followers of Jesus about himself. His healing ministry is primarily to be understood in the specific context of his Messianic, and therefore unique, mission. His healings and exorcisms provided opportunities to reveal his divine authority over the Jewish Law, in reinstating outcasts within society whilst providing them also with a relationship with God, in initiating the Kingdom and in the creation of opportunities for belief in Jesus, sufficient to give eternal life.

- As such, the healings are to be recognized as having an integrally important pedagogical function. Rather than assuming a direct line between Jesus' practice and healing today, the uniqueness of his ministry should be recognized and affirmed. Rather than viewing Jesus as a healing archetype, the evidence dictates that his healing ministry was unique.

- Jesus' ministry of healing and exorcism is worthy of ongoing consideration. His love and grace are to be marvelled at; his person and mission are to be the objects of our humble attention, inevitably filling us with wonder that such majesty chooses to minister to mere humans. At times, first-century onlookers thought his activity meaningless, while others thought him a magician or a madman. But to millions of those who have come to know him as the Son of God, he is none other than the Saviour of the world who gives hope to the hopeless and wholeness to all.

- Believers today are to be encouraged to present the healings and exorcisms of Jesus not primarily in the context of healing meetings or to simply remind believers of Jesus' healing power, but in order to exalt his person as the Saviour who came as God in the flesh. A study of his restorative ministry will lead to a greater perception of his majesty and authority. As the stories motivated the original readers to ask 'Is he God?' the modern reader is similarly encouraged to read them in the context of their historical setting and realise just how certain the answer is: 'Yes, he is.'

- Lessons may be drawn from the healing ministry of Jesus that can be usefully applied in contemporary healing settings, but cautious sensitivity needs to be applied in presenting the healing ministry of Jesus as a model for healing praxis today.

4. Healing in Acts

Introduction

The book of Acts is thought by many to act as a picture of Christianity functioning as it was intended to, with people coming to faith in the context of an explosion of signs and wonders throughout the Roman Empire. This portrayal, however, needs some qualification. It is true that many people came to faith and that signs and wonders were witnessed. However, by the end of the first century, Christians were still a very small minority of the population of the Empire. The words describing the success of Paul were often offered by those seeking to undermine his work. Thus, his enemies exaggerated his influence in order to present it as evidence of his threat to the status quo (Acts 17:6, 19:26). It is also to be noted that these early years were times of suffering and persecution for the believers. Not only were they being rejected by society as a whole (1 Pet. 1:6, 4:12), but doubts were beginning to creep in relating to their newfound faith, resulting in some people considering reverting to their previous beliefs (Heb. 2:1, 10:32–38). The sermons in Acts reflect some of these tensions, as do the letters of Paul.

There are relatively few accounts of supernatural healings in Acts, despite the fact that the events reflected in the book cover many years. Also, the vast majority described are achieved through the ministry of Peter and Paul. To suggest that healings were the norm would not be reflective of the message of Acts. Similarly, only one exorcism is described, and even that does not occur immediately on being encountered. Given the fact that the book of Acts is a survey of the history of the early church covering about thirty years, it is important to determine why the author included the particular miracles recorded and why he presented them as he did. It is also of interest to note that while healings in Luke form 12 per cent of the total verses, in Acts this is reduced to 4.5 per cent (in Pauline literature, the number reduces considerably more). This does not necessarily mean that healings were coming to an end in the early years of the church, but it might indicate a different priority in their being recorded. As with the authors of the Gospels, the author of Acts chooses to record healings for specific purposes, and it is to this issue that we now turn.

Significant Questions

Why did Luke record healing stories in Acts?

A number of answers may be offered for this important question:

- It is possible that especially in the early years of the church it was more appropriate to encourage the young believers by recording healing stories. Thus, they were able to benefit from the awareness that the one to whom they had dedicated their lives was a miracle-working God.

- It is also possible that Luke intended to demonstrate the value of healings in evangelistic contexts. However, although the healings achieved by Peter do result in belief on the part of some of the onlookers, this is not often replicated in the healing ministry of Paul. The healings achieved by Paul mainly resulted in either opposition or misunderstanding by those who observed what had occurred, sometimes resulting in them assuming that he was a god or giving him gifts. Nevertheless, the healings did create interest in the message of the Gospel and presented Jesus as being more significant than his competitors.

- What is clear from the book of Acts is that, as in the Gospels, the author does not provide a healing methodology that may easily be emulated by others; neither does he indicate that many believers were involved in a healing ministry nor that the potential of a healing ministry is available to every or any believer. Similarly, there is little to indicate that miracles of healing are achieved as a result of the Spirit. In this, he presents a healing ministry similar to that of Jesus, where the Spirit functions in a prophetic role with regard to Jesus, rather than in a miracle-working capacity.

- However, Luke does have an agenda in his provision of healing accounts and prominent motifs are visible. The key issue appears to be for the reader to recognize the healing authority of the Apostles, or at least Peter and Paul, often presented in parallel. Thus, their first healings (achieved in the presence of other Apostles, namely John and Barnabas, respectively) are of paralyzed men, afflicted from birth, the healings being achieved by a command and resulting in opposition. Both achieve a resurrection (9:36–43,

20:9–12) and their final healings are uniquely achieved by prayer (9:40, 28:8). The important aspects to be identified in the healings recorded in Acts are:

(i) The involvement of the Apostles (2:43, 5:12), mainly Peter (3:1–10, 4:30 [with John], 5:15, 9:32–35,36–43) and Paul (14:8–10,19f., 16:16–18, 19:11–20, 20:9–12, 28:3–6,7–9 [with Barnabas, 14:3, 15:12]).

(ii) The use of the name of Jesus (3:6,16, 4:10,30, 9:34, 16:16–23, 19:11).

(iii) The use of hands (9:12–19, 14:3, 19:11, 20:10, 28:4,8).

(iv) The use of a command (3:6, 9:34,40, 14:10).

(v) The immediacy of the restoration (3:7, 9:18,34,40, 14:10, 16:18, 28:6).

(vi) The variety of response: fear (2:43, 5:13), wonder (3:10, 8:13), belief (5:14, 8:6, 9:32,42), joy (8:8), opposition (14:4,19, 16:19), misunderstanding (14:11–13, 28:6,9,10).

Why did Luke record the healing stories related to Peter and Paul?

• The healings confirmed Peter and Paul as successful healers and valid messengers, Peter to the Jews, Paul to the Gentiles. In that respect, they functioned prophetically and evangelistically.

• The healings confirmed their apostolic status, as they also validated the status of Jesus (Lk. 7:20–22; Acts 2:22). Luke (Acts 10:38) records that God anointed Jesus with the Holy Spirit and power as a result of which Jesus healed all who were oppressed by the devil. The healings were identified as affirming the ministry of Jesus. So also, the healings achieved by the Apostles affirmed them and their ministries (11:26).

The healings also established the continuity from Jesus to the Apostles, their function being to affirm the latter as those who were entrusted with the responsibility of proclaiming a new era of salvation, as they did in the ministry of Jesus.

• The healings confirmed the Apostles as bearing the hallmarks of Jesus. They were not just healers; they were healers in the mould of Jesus. This is noted by Luke in many ways:

(i)   As Jesus performed signs and wonders (2:22), so also, they were described as performing them (2:43, 4:16,22,30, 5:12, 14:3, 15:12). The healings were not only miraculous physical restorations; they also pointed to something even more important. The miraculous ministry of Jesus provided a foretaste of the new Kingdom that he was establishing, demonstrated his authority and authenticated the revelation he brought. They were acts of redemption and the Apostles were presented as following his agenda.

(ii) Their ability to heal did not necessarily validate them as followers of Jesus, for pagan healings also occurred in that era. However, the way they healed did, and Luke records them healing as Jesus did. The guidelines of James 5:14–18 are strangely absent. Instead, Luke depicts the Apostles following a different agenda, one represented by Jesus' healing ministry. Thus, Peter and Paul heal with the use of their hands, issue commands and achieve immediate restorations, as did Jesus.

(iii) As the healings in the Gospels provided evidence of Jesus' identification with God in that God is encountered in his miraculous activity, so also

Jesus is encountered in the healings of the Apostles. The work of the Apostles is still the work of Jesus … God is the agent of both.

(iv) There were similar varied reactions to the healings as reflected in the healings of Jesus, ranging from joy, discipleship, the praise of God (3:9) to fear (2:43), persecution and rejection (5:17,18). Similarly, in the healing ministry of the Apostles, there was no unambiguous reference to the issue of sin as a possible cause of the sickness, no request to repent for sins that may have caused the sickness to occur, and no mention of oil, all of which are referred to in James 5:14–18 but none of which were reflected in the ministry of Jesus. Luke, in his Gospel, is particularly desirous of stressing the teaching role of Jesus, and this is also reflected in the healing accounts related to Peter and Paul (Jesus: 10:36–38; Apostles: 4:29; Peter: 14:8–10; Paul: 19:10–12). Peter and Paul are reminiscent of Jesus.

(v) It is at this point that the significance of the Apostles' healings may be further appreciated. The healings did not just validate them and their ministry; they are also to be understood as validating the person and ministry of Jesus in the present in so far as the miracles are presented as being the ongoing work of the risen Lord, albeit through the Apostles.

Acts 1:1 indicates that while the Gospel of Luke introduced the beginning of the acts and teaching of Jesus, Acts completed the story, but the latter is still a reflection of the acts and works of Jesus. To assume that the Apostles are the focus of the book of Acts is to miss the point.

Although Paul and Peter are paralleled, Jesus is viewed as being central to both of their ministries.

Many parallels may be drawn between the ministries of Paul and Jesus[1] and between Peter and Jesus.[2] It is not necessary to doubt the historical value of the healings in Acts and to assume that they are the creation of the author who has used his skills to create the Apostles in the likeness of Jesus. Rather, the healings described in Acts are to be accepted as authentic while the author has chosen those recorded to draw a parallel with those achieved by Jesus.

What is to be determined is the reason for this parallelism. As has been suggested, the author is seeking to indicate that the Apostles functioned as did Jesus in order to prove that the heavenly Jesus is still functioning through his designated followers. The ministry of Jesus is continuing.

Thus, the readers are directed back to Jesus, as are the observers of miracles (3:12,16). Not only are the Apostles imitating Jesus' ministry, but they are also demonstrating his present activity

---

[1] Jesus cast out demons (Lk. 4:31–37), also Paul (Acts 16:16–18); both Jesus and Paul cured fevers (Lk. 4:38; Acts 28:9), followed in each case by many others coming for healing, service being offered to them; Jesus heals a lame man (Lk. 5:17–26), so does Paul (Acts 14:8–18); power left Jesus, resulting in healings (Lk. 6:19), also Paul (Acts 19:11f.); Jesus raised the dead (Lk. 7:11–17), so also Paul (Acts 20:7–12); touching Jesus' garment achieved healing (Lk. 8:44), also Paul (Acts 19:12). Jesus (Lk. 19:45–48) and Paul (Acts 21:26) enter the Temple on their entries into Jerusalem; both are seized by a mob (Lk. 22:54; Acts 21:30); both are slapped by the priest's assistants (Lk. 22:63f.; Acts 23:2); both are involved in four trials (Lk. 22:26, 23:1,8,13;

amongst them. He is still achieving signs and wonders, but this time, it is through the Apostles. The importance of the healings in Acts is to demonstrate that as Jesus indicated his authority in the Gospel of Luke by his healings, so his authority is still evident in the life of the early church. Rather than the Ascension signaling an absent Christ, the book of Acts identifies a present Christ functioning through the Apostles (16:7), as he said he would, doing what he did when he was in his physical body. Paul writes similarly in Romans 15:18,19 when he describes Christ working through him … in signs and wonders.

Who else is recorded as healing in Acts and why?

Philip (8:6–8,13) and Stephen (6:8) are also recorded as engaging in 'signs and wonders'. Ananias (9:12–19) is the only other person identified in a healing narrative, though it appears that he is less significant than the one healed, Saul, who will be Paul, the Apostle.

It is important to recognize the quality of these people. Stephen and Philip are two of the Seven, chosen because

Footnote 1 continued

Acts 23, 24, 25, 26); both have a Herod involved in their trials (Lk. 23:6–12; Acts 25:13 – 26:32); both have a centurion act positively towards them (Lk. 23:47; Acts 27:3,43); both their ministries conclude in the context of the fulfilment of Scripture (Lk. 24; Acts 28).

[2] Jesus heals a lame man (Lk. 5:17–26), so does Peter (Acts 3: 1–10); power left Jesus, resulting in healings (Lk. 6:19), so also did people expect the same of Peter (Acts 5:15); Jesus raised the dead (Lk. 7:11–17), so also Peter (Acts 9:36–43); Jesus cast out demons (Lk. 4:31–37), so also Peter (Acts 5:16).

of their character, wisdom (6:3) and the presence of the Spirit in their lives (6:5,6). They are representative of those with leadership qualities. Rather than view the Seven as undertaking less important responsibilities (i.e. simply waiting on tables), their role of caring for widows (6:1) is reflected elsewhere by Luke where he refers positively to widows (Lk. 2:36–38, 4:25–27, 7:11–17, 21:1–4), indicating their importance. Similarly, the importance of service as a demonstration of true discipleship is also mentioned elsewhere by Luke (Lk. 22:14–19 and especially 22:27). The qualities in their lifestyles, as a result of which they were chosen to be part of the Seven, demonstrate their high calling. For God to use them in this service comes as no surprise. The church functions in the context of holiness and Spirit-empowered living and both Stephen and Philip reflected these features.

A number of comments may be made that provide possible reasons for their inclusion by Luke in the healing narratives:

- They are recorded in succession with no miracles being recorded by anyone else in the section. As such, they form a literary bridge, signaling that a transition is being developed during which Luke moves from a description concentrating on most of the healings of Peter to those of Paul.

- Unlike Peter, they have not received a personal commissioning from Jesus. The stage is set for someone else who also has not received a personal commission from the pre-Ascension Jesus either. And so, the martyrdom of Stephen ushers the name of Saul into the narrative.

- More importantly, as with Peter and Paul, they defined new evangelistic missions. In each, as with Jesus, the healings that took place in their missions functioned as effective stimuli, encouraging people to turn to faith in Christ. Stephen, a Hellenist, became the first martyr at the hands of the Jews to whom the Gospel had been preached, signaling the development of the Gospel being presented elsewhere, initially in Samaria (8:5–26).

This is followed in the narrative by the mission to Samaria by Philip (8:4–8,13,26–40), in fulfilment of Acts 1:8. Philip also preached to the Ethiopian eunuch, a God-fearing Gentile from a nation recognized as being on the fringes of the world.

The progress of the Gospel from the heart of Jerusalem to the Gentiles was defined by Luke in the context of the activity of the miraculous, again reminiscent of the ministry of Jesus. In that respect, Luke achieved an important objective: healings were to be recognized as definitions of authority of the gospel and its presentation to the Gentile world. The evangelistic mission of Jesus outlined in Luke's Gospel was outworked through the Apostles in Acts and, as with Jesus, their evangelism was associated with healings.

• As Peter and Paul, they are also portrayed as prophets, the signs and wonders they performed being indicative of their prophetic status. Stephen is presented as functioning as an OT prophet by Luke, in 'power' (6:8) and 'the Holy Spirit' (6:5), engaging in 'wonders and signs' (6:8). He is described as having the face of an angel (6:15), mentioned immediately after a reference to Moses (6:14). Philip demonstrates his prophetic credentials also. He 'was full of the Spirit and wisdom' (6:3), performed signs (8:6,13), healed people and cast out demons (8:7), was visited by an angel (8:26) and was miraculously transported by the Spirit from the desert to Azotus (8:39,40), as similarly happened to the prophets Elijah (1 Kgs.

18:12) and Ezekiel (Ezek. 11:24). In this prophetic function, Stephen and Philip follow in the footsteps of Jesus (Lk. 1:35).

- Most importantly, they are also explicitly reminiscent of Jesus.
  - (i)   Philip's preaching is reminiscent of Jesus (Acts 8:7). It is characteristically described as comprising 'good news about the Kingdom of God' (8:12). As with Jesus, Philip's preaching is accompanied by exorcisms and healings (8:6,7,13) and much joy (8:8).
  - (ii) The qualities of Stephen, namely grace and power (6:8, 7:10,22), are, with wisdom, paralleled in Luke 2:40,52, where the wisdom, grace and favour of Jesus are mentioned. Stephen is accused with the same charges leveled at Jesus, concerning the Temple (Lk. 21:6; Acts 6:13,14). Parallels may also be noted in that both Jesus and Stephen spoke as inspired by the Spirit (Lk. 4:18,19; Acts 7:10), their words resulting in opposition (Lk. 4:28,29; Acts 7:54–58). Many other links between Jesus and Stephen indicate that the author is seeking to establish the same message as he did with Peter and Paul, namely that the ascended Jesus is not absent from his church.[3] He is still present and functioning miraculously through the church.

---

[3] The link between miracles and preaching (Lk. 4:31ff.; Acts 6:8,10); the false witnesses (Mt. 26:60; Acts 6:11); their accusations concerning the ways their opponents persecuted the prophets (Lk. 11:47–50; Acts 7:52); their prayers requesting forgiveness for their accusers (Lk. 23:34; Acts 7:60); the words used by them both before their deaths, relating to the Son of Man being at the right hand of God (Lk. 22:69; Acts 7:56); and

What lessons may be learned from the first healing story in Acts (3:1–16,20–27)?

Given that this is the first and longest healing narrative in Acts and that the significance of the miracle is developed in such detail by the author (3:1 – 4:22), it deserves our attention. It is significant to note that the first recorded healing in Acts is of a paralyzed man, such people being included in those who were invited to the banquet described by Jesus in Luke 14:13. People with such a disability were excluded from the priesthood (Lev. 21: 16–18); that he was at the Temple gate probably indicates that he was not allowed inside, given the prohibitions against some ill folk from entering the Temple.

This account provides a useful example of the Apostles functioning in the context of the mission of Jesus, incorporating a number of aspects common to the healings of Jesus, especially in relation to the healing of

---

Footnote 3 continued

while Jesus commends his spirit to his father (Lk. 23:46), Stephen commits his spirit to Jesus (Acts 7:59). As Stephen is described as being 'full of the Holy Spirit' (Acts 6:5) before his test with the religious opposition, so Jesus is presented as 'full of the Holy Spirit' (Lk. 4:1) before his test with the devil. As Jesus is presented as amazing his hearers in the Temple (Lk. 2:47), so also the opposition could not compete with the wisdom of Stephen (Acts 6:10; it is significant to note that wisdom was also characteristic of Jesus [Lk. 2:40,52, 7:35, 11:31, 21:15]). Stephen's referral of the title 'Son of Man' to Jesus (7:56) is unique outside the Gospels as is the fact that he describes the Son of Man as standing at the right hand of God, as opposed to sitting, a fact mentioned twice in the narrative (7:55f.). Stephen is not simply functioning as a follower of Jesus, but as one who is specially affirmed by him in his particular role (as described in Lk. 12:8).

the paralytic in Luke 5:17–26. The major motifs of the healings recorded in Acts are all featured in this account.

The story itself is about a man, described as paralyzed from birth, over forty years previously (4:22), who had on a daily basis been carried and laid at the Beautiful Gate in order to beg. On seeing the Apostles, Peter and John, he asks for alms, Luke commenting on the fact that he expected to receive something from them, though he expresses no expectancy of healing. Peter, after asking the man to look at them, commands him to walk 'in the name of Jesus Christ of Nazareth', and lifts the man to his feet, whereupon his healing is achieved immediately and completely, resulting in his praising God, walking and jumping up and down.

The use of a command, the immediacy and complete nature of the healing are reminiscent of the healing ministry of Jesus, though other elements also focus the attention of the reader on Jesus. There are also significant parallels located in the wider contexts. Thus, while this healing is introduced after the first account of new believers being added to the church (2:47), Luke 5:17–26 is recorded after Jesus' calling of the Twelve; both result in the first reference to opposition by religious leaders; both lead to statements concerning the authority of Jesus to save.

Furthermore, Luke presents the healings being achieved with two significant elements, either of which are sufficient to remind the reader of the person and healing ministry of Jesus: namely, the name of Jesus and/ or the use of touch in the healing process.

The significance of the use of a name
Although Jesus does not use a name in his healing of the paralytic in Luke 5:17–26, the healing is not to be contrasted with that described in Acts 3. On the contrary, this

is the only significant difference and, given that the use of the name focuses attention on the person of Jesus, its incorporation by Peter more closely relates the healing with that achieved by Jesus. The relationship with Jesus is emphasized most importantly by the fact that the healing is described as having been achieved by Jesus, this feature being recorded no less than seven times (3:6,13,16 [twice], 4:10 [twice], 4:30).

In 4:10, Peter informs his audience that the healing of the paralytic was achieved in the name of Jesus. The focus is concentrated on the fact that the healing is achieved through the medium of a name, in particular, the name of Jesus, this being mentioned four times in the ensuing verses, the person of Jesus being glorified as a result (3:13). Referring back to this healing, the discussion by the Jewish religious hierarchy (4:7) involved an identification of the healing power with the name, suggesting that, in their understanding, they are synonymous. The command (4:17,18) that the Apostles do not speak or teach 'in the name of Jesus' again suggests that the notions of authority and power are integral to the phrase. To call upon the name of the Lord is to invoke the protection and power of the Lord. His name functions as a representation of his power.

Luke is not suggesting that the name is a substitute of the risen Jesus as if it were achieving the miracle; he is simply indicating that the miracle is achieved by the one who bears that name, even though he is not present in bodily form. Although Peter, in his sermon (4:12), quotes from Joel 2:32, where the identity of the Lord is Yahweh, in 4:18 the name bearer is identified as being Jesus. The importance of the person of Jesus is thus developed by Luke in his narrative. He is the Lord, discharging all the functions of Yahweh in the OT, by way of revelation, salvation and healing.

The significance of touch
The fact that Peter lifts (by the right hand, reminiscent of Lk. 6:6) the man to his feet is also of significance as the use of the hand in healing was frequent in the ministry of Jesus, an issue that has been explored earlier.

The context and aftermath
The immediate aftermath of the healing is of the description of the actions of the man who was healed. The description of his walking, leaping and praising God (3:7) is reminiscent of Isaiah 35:6. There, the bringer of salvation is Yahweh. Luke has in mind a different Saviour, namely Jesus, who functions as did Yahweh. The healing should not be interpreted in a vacuum but also be seen as part of a more comprehensive context. Thus, the fact that the healing is twice described as a sign (4:16,22) begs the question, 'Of what?' It functions fundamentally as a Christological sign.

The miracle results in wonder and amazement on the part of those who witnessed the transformation in the man and provides Peter with an opportunity to preach a sermon concerning Jesus that Luke records in some length. In it, Peter points to Jesus as the originator of their power (3:16, 4:7,10,30). Crucially, he widens the significance of the name of Jesus in that the one who bears that name is not just the source of healing but also of salvation (4:12). Elsewhere, Luke uses the term 'save' (*sōzō*) to describe physical healing (8:48,50, 23:35), as here (4:9), though he more often uses it to describe a salvation of a different nature (7:50, 8:36, 17:19, 18:26, 19:10). Although the term is used initially to describe the physical transformation of the man, it is soon used to refer to the spiritual salvation available through Jesus (4:12). The story takes on its appropriate significance when it is interpreted as a Christocentric signpost, not merely a remarkable healing, identifying Jesus as the one with authority to provide wholeness, of which physical healing is only a partial realization. In this regard, it is reminiscent of the healing ministry of Jesus. Thus, Peter explains who Jesus is (3:13–15) and that God resurrected him (v. 15) before referring to his part in the restoration of the paralyzed man.

As with the healings of Jesus, this healing demands a response, and Peter presents the challenge forcibly (3:12–26, 4:8–12). The response, as with Jesus, is varied. Luke records the people wondering (3:10) and later praising God (4:21), the latter characteristic being replicated by the healed man (3:9,10). Five thousand men come to faith (4:4) and the believers pray for boldness to preach, resulting in their being filled with the Spirit (4:23–31). However, the religious opposition imprisoned the Apostles (4:2), despite their recognizing that they had witnessed a 'notable sign' (4:16). As Jesus before them who, as a result of his healings, was deemed to be a prophet but was rejected, so the Apostles undergo the same experience.

The person and authority of Jesus are emphasized through the healing ministry of the Apostles. As with Jesus, an outcast is integrated; also, the one healed receives spiritual wholeness (3:9,16, 4:14) resulting in an opportunity for a response, the people realizing 'that they had been with Jesus' (4:14–18,24,25).

The main lessons to be gleaned from the story as told by Luke appear to be:

- A recognition of the fact that although Jesus is in his ascended state, he still functions on earth, as reflected in this healing, which is reminiscent of his earthly healing ministry.

- Healings are valuable catalysts for determining one's assessment of Jesus; they point to him.

- Physical healing in an evangelistic setting, as in this narrative, is anticipated by the author as being the potential precursor of a transformation that has spiritual implications.

Does the book of Acts provide a pattern for healing today?

It is very difficult to be certain whether the author of Acts intended to provide a pattern for healing for future believers partly because so few people are presented by him as being involved in healings. Those who are involved function as leaders in the church. However, it is not necessary to assume that only leaders can be involved in healings; indeed, James and Paul anticipate all believers as potentially being involved. It would be apposite to note that healings continued to be experienced in the earliest years of the church and were appropriate in evangelism, though they did not only occur in these settings.

It is difficult to determine a consistent healing process in the ministries of Peter and Paul since the healings were achieved in a variety of ways. In 28:3–6, for example, Luke records Paul being protected from the poisonous effects of a snake in the absence of prayer, the use of the name of Jesus and the laying on of hands, while there is no reference to the concept of faith. Paul simply shakes the snake off his hand and is unharmed. Nevertheless, some comments may be offered.

The name of Jesus
The use of the name of Jesus in healing is regularly recorded in the book of Acts (3:6,16, 4:10, 9:34). The clearest derivation of this usage is located in the promises

by Jesus to his disciples concerning the efficacy of his name (Jn. 14:13,14, 15:16, 16:24). The person who prays in the name of Jesus is expressing trust in him to achieve the request, the outworking potentially as immediate and as effective as if Jesus were achieving the miracle; the person and the name of Jesus are thus indistinguishable (Acts 4:12, 5:41, 9:16, 15:26, 21:13). For Luke, the name of Jesus is integral to his teaching, for it is due to Jesus that restoration was achieved. The name of Jesus is understood to be representative of his person. Similarly, in Acts 16:18, the inclusion of the name in a command ('I charge you in the name of Jesus Christ to come out of her'), followed by the obedient response of the demon ('it came out'), emphasizes this connection with power. This issue is explored later in the analysis of the guidelines offered by James.

Although physically absent, the risen Jesus is present and the perspective of Luke is to endorse this by the use of the name of Jesus, most clearly presented in 9:34 ('Jesus Christ heals you'). To use the name of Jesus in prayer for healing today is appropriate as a means of identifying the source of healing power and also as a reminder that it is *his* authority that results in the healing taking place.

The role of faith
The role of faith in the context of healing is rare in Acts, only mentioned in 3:16 and 14:9. There was no expectation of healing on the part of the paralyzed man in the account recorded in Acts 3. Luke notes that, having asked for money, he only expected to receive money. Similarly, there was no request for healing, neither was the healing achieved as the result of the power or piety of the Apostles (v. 12). It is to be assumed that the confidence of Peter to assume that the man would be healed

was due to God having informed him that this was to occur. This feature is described by Paul as the receiving of a gift of faith, an assurance that, in this context, God would achieve a restorative miracle. Peter is thus given prior notice of this fact and responds to this affirmation from God by commanding the man to stand up and helping him to do so. Thus, on this occasion, Peter does not pray but simply expects the healing to occur as in 9:32–35. Faith that is identified as being imparted by God as assurance that the person prayed for is to be restored is important in healing scenarios. Believers today should look to God for guidance as to his will when praying for people and be prepared for his gift of faith in the context of their prayer. This gift provides assurance that their prayer or action is in line with the will of God. It is God's way of letting us know that we are operating as he would wish us to do.

The value of prayer

When confronted with the dead body of Tabitha (9:36–43), Peter prays before any restoration occurs. This probably indicates his desire to ascertain the will of God in this situation. After all, this is the first recorded resurrection referred to in Acts. After the prayer, he commands Tabitha to rise, indicating that he is responding to advice divinely imparted in the time of prayer. That she is restored demonstrates that he has not functioned presumptuously but in accordance with the will of God.

Similarly, in 28:7–9, Paul is recorded as healing Publius' father, prayer and the laying on of hands being aspects of the cure of the fever and dysentery. The presence of prayer in this final recorded healing of Paul is unusual, though it is also present in the final recorded miracle of Peter and may indicate that Paul, as Peter, only functioned in the miraculous in response to the commission of God, here provided through prayer. For believers today, prayer should be recognized as having value not just as a means of bringing one's request to God but also as an opportunity to hear from God and, in particular, to receive guidance as to how to pray most appropriately.

The value of touch
Both Peter and Paul sometimes touched those who were restored. In 20:9–12, Eutychus is restored following an embrace by Paul, while Tabitha was helped to sit up by Peter taking her hand. Touch was an important part of the ministry of Jesus, as has been explored earlier. It can be appropriately incorporated into current healing practice as a sign that while physical hands are laid on a person, the more powerful hands of the Lord are also present to provide wholeness.

Why is only one exorcism recorded in Acts and what is its significance?

Acts 16:16–18 provide a description of the only specific exorcism recorded in Acts. The exorcism is achieved by Paul, who uses the name of Jesus Christ, resulting in the demon being immediately expelled. Luke describes the girl as having a spirit of divination (*puthona*). The god Apollo, who was associated with the pronouncement of oracles, was worshipped at Delphi. Puthon was the name of a snake that inhabited Delphi, functioning as a symbol of the underworld and of Apollo in particular. It was believed that the original snake had been killed by Apollo who was thus named Pythian Apollo.

The evil spirit attempted to demonstrate its authority by revealing its ability to identify Paul as a servant of God. It was not supporting the mission of Paul but probably intending to damage it, perhaps by linking it with the occult in the minds of the listeners or by simply being a constant and irritating, albeit affirmatory, heckler.

The force of the emotional outburst on the part of Paul is strong (16:18). The term used to describe Paul's feelings (*diaponeomai*) is also used in 4:2 to describe the annoyance felt by the priests and Sadducees due to the continuing preaching of the Apostles. The irritation felt by Paul is probably because this activity on the part of the girl had been continuing for many days, though he may have suddenly got tired of the constant intrusion by a demonic source. Why he did not deal with the demon earlier is a question not addressed by Luke. It is probable that Paul dealt with the spirit only when it began to hinder his ministry. Indeed, it may have unwittingly served a valid purpose for the Apostle, attracting people to him. Given the worldview of the people, which entertained the possibility of truth being imparted by such diviners, the proclamation may have encouraged people to listen to Paul as one who was apparently being affirmed by such an authentic source, associated with the great Oracle at Delphi.

The fact that this is the only recorded exorcism in Acts is worthy of comment, especially as it contrasts with the ministry of Jesus. Given that Paul's ministry took him to places where such occultic phenomena were more common than in Jewish communities, given the religious diversities and occultic activity in the former, this is all the more unusual. A number of conclusions may be proposed:

- The ministry of Jesus with regard to demonic activity does not appear to be replicated in the early church as far as the record of Acts is concerned. Individual exorcisms are not recorded elsewhere in the NT. It appears that they were particularly important in the ministry of Jesus as a sign of the in-breaking of the new Kingdom he came to establish.

- That Paul removes the demon 'in the name of Jesus' indicates that the action is appropriate and legitimized by the incorporation of the name and the immediacy of the expulsion.

- In the light of a great deal of interest in the demonic by a variety of Christians, it is instructive to note the paucity of such comment by the writers in the NT outside the ministry of Jesus. That is not to suggest that exorcisms did not occur; they did, and Luke records this in Acts 8:7 and 19:12. It is conceivable that they occurred regularly, but were not commented on individually. A parallel may be drawn with some contemporary African and Asian contexts where exorcism is a frequent phenomenon, and as such warrants little comment because of its regularity. The one incident in the book of Acts need not be necessarily taken to indicate a rare example of an exorcism in the early church. On the contrary, rather than simply recording an exorcism, Luke is demonstrating a more sobering fact concerning the supernatural opposition leveled against Paul.

- The story is more important than it might appear. Although the exorcism is recorded in one verse, the following twenty-two verses record the con-sequences. This is not a story recording the demise of one evil spirit; it is a story recording the potential death of the Apostles and the demise of their mission in Philippi. The focus of the story is not on the authority of Paul to cast out a demon but on the authority of God to overcome all obstacles to the mission of his delegated messengers, whether they be demons (16:18), mobs (16:19), rulers (16:20,21), physical abuse (16:22–24) or prison (16:24). Following the exorcism and all the negative consequences for the Apostles, concluding with their imprisonment, an earthquake is recorded as shaking all the doors off their hinges in the prison, the chains on the Apostles are loosed (16:26), the jailors become believers (16:31–34), the rulers apologize to the Apostles (16:39) and the believers are encouraged (16:40). The demon may have been infuriating but God was actually in charge.

- The question hangs in the air as to whether Paul should have carried out the exorcism. Would his ministry have been unimpeded if he had ignored the girl? Luke presents the subtlety of the opposition force against Paul. Paul is in a dilemma. If he ignores the spirit, it will act as a constant irritant. If he exorcizes it, it will result in the truncation of his mission in Philippi. Luke informs his readers that the results of the exorcism resulted in the Apostles being beaten and imprisoned. It appears that the spirit had won a decisive battle in its suicidal attack. In removing the girl from bondage, the Apostles were themselves bound.

  However, the story ends with the jailer's family becoming believers and being baptized and the Apostles are released, with a public apology. Although the opposition forces initially seemed to have won the battle, Luke is desirous of demonstrating that they were pawns in the hands of the one who was supervising the destiny of Paul. This is less a story of an exorcism of a spirit and more a record of a malevolent mastermind who seeks to destroy the mission of Paul; but even more importantly, the confirmation that Paul is guarded by a superior power.

- Outside of the Synoptics, the guidance offered by other NT writers relating to the demonic is that the most appropriate elements in responding to such forces include being filled with the Spirit (Eph. 5:18), taking advantage of the resources of God which are available to believers (Eph. 6:13–18) and resisting temptation (1 Pet. 5:8). In Romans 16:20, Paul encourages Christian behaviour, as a result of which God will disarm Satan. Similarly, self-control (1 Cor. 7:5; Eph. 4:26,27) and forgiveness (2 Cor. 2:11) are viewed as antidotes to Satan's measures against the believer. Paul deduces that the alien powers are subservient to Christ (Col. 2:10), were originally created for him (Col. 1:16) and were disarmed by him at the cross (Col. 2:15). At the same time, Paul is aware of their malevolence (Eph. 2:2, 6:12) and calls for believers to resist them, mainly through the ministry of love within the Christian community (Eph. 4:1–6, 5:1,2) and the resources made available by God (Eph. 6:10–18).

Is there any value in the use of handkerchiefs or cloths in healings?

In Acts 19:11–20, Luke records the fact that miracles, described as 'extraordinary', were achieved by Paul. He also comments on the fact that bandannas or sweat rags, used to prevent sweat running into the eyes, were carried to the sick, after having been used by Paul, resulting in the sick being healed and evil spirits being exorcized.

These were unusual days in which remarkable activities were taking place, so unusual that they were described as being extraordinary miracles. There is no suggestion that they should be viewed as paradigms for other eras or for the use of prayer cloths today. It should not be assumed that any healing properties resided in the cloths themselves or that they provided points of contact necessary for healings to occur. It was simply a reported event in the life of the church that Luke records with no other comment or declaration that it should happen again.

It is probable that this event reveals more about the nature of the people referred to in this story. Paul was in Ephesus, a city used to magical activity (Acts 19:19) and acquainted with the belief that supernatural properties could be transmitted via objects. Thus, charms and special letters, known as Ephesian Letters, were purchased in the city, placed in small metal tubes or lockets and hung around the neck in the hope that disasters would be averted and desires would be actualized.

Similarly, Acts 5:15 records an extraordinary incident relating to the ministry of Peter. The belief of people in the power of the Apostles was such that Luke records them as laying the sick in the streets in the hope that Peter's shadow would fall on them, it being viewed as having therapeutic power. Luke does not record that anybody was healed because of this belief, simply using the fact to record the extent of their readiness to believe that healings were possible. It is conceivable that had such an unusual event occurred, he would have recorded it. Nevertheless, he does record that all those who were brought for healing were healed. The result of this activity, as recorded by Luke, is varied. Some feared to join the believers while others held them in high honour (5:13); many became believers (5:14) though, because of jealousy, the Sadducees arrested the Apostles and imprisoned them (5:17f.). As with Jesus, healings had a varied response, resulting in belief and rejection.

Both accounts describe unusual events and, while they may not necessarily be repeated, it does remind us that God, in his sovereignty, is capable of providing extra-ordinary miracles, especially of value in certain cultural contexts.

Implications for the Contemporary Church

- Luke does not record a number of characteristics related to healing that are reflected in the guidelines of James. These include oil, elders, the righteousness of the one praying, the significance of sin to the sickness or repentance to the healing, and the prayer of faith. There is also very little mention of prayer (9:36–43, 28:7–9) or faith (14:8–11) in Acts. He presents a different framework for healing from that offered in James 5:13–18.

- The healings in Acts, to a very large degree, replicate the pattern of those achieved by Jesus. The Apostles did not emulate the mission of Jesus, for that is unique, but they did demonstrate the presence and the person of Jesus through their healings. They achieved this, in part, in the way that the healings were reminiscent of his healing ministry. As such, Jesus is seen to have permeated their ministry, their healing praxis being evocative of his. Luke's record shows that the healings reflect the ongoing presence of Jesus in the ministry of the church.

- The author of Acts desires to encourage his readers to recognize that Jesus is still present despite his bodily absence and that he still functions in authority. The reasons for this are paramount and twofold:

(i)   The author directs the reader to the person of Jesus, focusing on his authority. To a sophisticated Gentile audience, used to the dominating authority of the Greek and Roman gods, such authority is a crucial marker. Luke stresses this theme in the final two chapters of Acts, which indicate the authority of the risen Lord. Despite the dangers of the sea voyage of Paul from Jerusalem across the Mediterranean Sea to Rome and all that occurred, he arrived safely, against all the odds, resulting in Luke concluding his narrative with the information that Paul was able to teach 'about the Lord Jesus Christ quite openly and *unhindered*' (28:31). Similarly, the healings demonstrate that the most feared enemies, sickness and death, are subservient to the authority of Jesus vested in followers of Jesus. Although alternative healers existed in the first century, the healings recorded in Acts demonstrate unique features, including the immediacy of restoration and an absence of ritualistic or magical elements. This quality of authority and power indicates the superior nature of the Lord to whom the believers have committed their lives. In a world that was determined by issues of power and authority, it was important that the new faith of the believers was identified as credible and authentic. This is partly demonstrated by the supernatural events occurring at the hands of the leaders of the Christian community.

(ii) The early church will soon, if not already, be experiencing the traumas that accompany persecution and lethargy. The message that the risen Lord is still functioning in authority is a timely message that needs to be documented for all concerned. Luke, in Acts, achieves this by building on his first work, his Gospel. In the latter, Jesus' healing ministry demonstrates the supremacy of his authority, indicating that he functions with divine authority with regard to major issues, including sickness and demonic influences. In Acts, Luke affirms Jesus as the risen authoritative Saviour who still lives and functions through his church. Although persecution will come and suffering will be experienced by believers, they will know that the one who also suffered at the hands of others when on this earth is amongst them. The resurrection did not signal an absent Jesus. He is still with believers; the healings are evidence of this.

• Notwithstanding the miracles of restoration that occurred in the early church, throughout church history, and particularly in the past decades, caution is appropriate if one attempts to glean a methodology of healing from the book of Acts. That is not because divine healings have ceased; they have not. However, the focus of the author has been to look back to Jesus, not forward to a Christian healing community in the future. That is not to suggest that a Christian healing community is illegitimate or not reflective of the ongoing work of Jesus. However, although divine healings are anticipated as an ongoing work of the church in the NT and beyond, the purpose of the author of Acts is not to prepare for it so much as to focus on the one who is central to it. The healings of Jesus are presented as continuing through the book of Acts, Jesus being central to both parts of the Luke–Acts continuum, the motif that pervades the whole relating to the authority of Jesus.

Thus, the healings described in Acts are similar to those of Jesus, presented in similar contexts and with similar consequences. Those achieving the healings are also presented in parallel with Jesus' ministry and lifestyle. In addition, there is a marked dissimilarity between the healing procedures presented in Acts and the guidelines offered by James. While James concentrates on prayer as that which achieves restoration, Acts concentrates on the person of Jesus as the one who initiates it.

- The guidelines for such an ongoing healing ministry are best located in James 5:13–18. That is not to undermine the authenticity of the miracles recorded in Acts or the reality of healings today. However, for a contemporary methodology of healing, the believer should look to Paul and his reference to the gifts of healings and to James.

  The book of Acts is intended to show the ongoing ministry of Jesus which 'he began to do' (Acts 1:1) in Luke's account of his ministry. The book of James is intended to show the ongoing ministry of the church. This contrast must not be presented too harshly as if there is a disparity between both writers. Rather, different lessons are being provided for their different audiences. Acts encourages the readers, drawing attention to the presence of Jesus as demonstrated by supernatural healings described. James encourages his readers to be involved in divinely achieved restorations. The message of both is complementary, not competitive.

- The contemporary church is as much in need of a consistent infusion of the truth that Jesus is present to encourage, guide, support and empower as was the early church. An increasingly secular world dominated by a postmodern, humanist agenda means that without a robust awareness of the presence of Jesus the church will be in danger of losing its focus and ability to grow. To be aware of the person and presence of Jesus is a crucial antidote to malevolent forces against it and a powerful resource for its authoritative stance in a world that is lost without it.

5. Healings and Suffering in Paul's Letters

Introduction

Paul does not mention the healings or exorcisms of Jesus; neither does he refer to them as being a model for the activities of believers. Instead, he refers to gifts of healings (1 Cor. 12:9,30) as well as the role of healers (1 Cor. 12:28). Similarly, miraculous healings are noticeable by their lack of centrality in the Pauline letters, though there are allusions to them in 1 Corinthians 2:4,5 and 1 Thessalonians 1:5. Miracles are referred to in 2 Corinthians 12:11,12 and in Romans 15:18,19 Paul refers to Christ working through him 'by the power of signs and wonders'.

Significant Questions

What are gifts of healings (1 Cor. 12:9)?

Although medical healing may be viewed as a gift of God, it is more likely that Paul is referring to super-natural healing by this term. Paul does not suggest that it is possible or advisable to request or develop a gift of healing. The distribution of gifts to believers is the role of the Spirit (1 Cor. 12:7,11), and although Paul recommends that believers earnestly desire the greater gifts (1 Cor. 12:31), he is here referring to those that are more likely to benefit the community in which one is situated at any given time. If one was in a situation where restoration to wholeness was being requested of God, it would be appropriate to ask the Spirit for an outpouring of this gift, though the response is always the responsibility of the Spirit who, as God, does all things well (Rom. 8:27,28). A number of explanations are suggested for these gifts:

- It is possible that the term refers to the individual gift of healing as received by an individual whose illness is removed. Thus, the person who is healed receives a gift of healing.

- Alternatively, it may refer to a supernatural capacity on the part of someone to heal some illnesses more than others. The fact that both words are presented in the plural may indicate that Paul is indicating different healing capabilities for various kinds of illnesses and diseases. Although some have claimed this to be a reflection of their own healing ministries, it begs the question as to what one would do if a particular restorative capacity was not available when someone with a different ailment was in need of ministry. It is also not reflected in the healing narratives in Acts nor in James 5:13–18.

- A further option is reflected in the suggestion that gifts of healings are best understood as descriptions of healings that occur through individuals as they minister to those who need restoration. Although it need not be assumed that such ability necessarily resides in a believer permanently, Paul does describe healers as existing in the church (1 Cor. 12:28). Such a definition may be applied to those who function in this gift more than other people. Paul does not give guidelines as to how these gifts operate; he simply assumes that they do. It may be deduced that those who have been used by God in this regard should function sensitively, always seeking to rely on the leading of the Spirit who bestows this gift on people as he wills (1 Cor. 12:4–11).

What is the relationship between the gift of faith and gifts of healings?

Both gifts are referred to in 1 Corinthians 12:9 and it is no coincidence that they are presented consecutively, for they are integrally related to each other. Both the faith and the power to heal are described as gifts, given by the Spirit.

Identity of faith

Faith is to be identified as believing in God in a particular situation. When God provides a promise in Scripture, the willingness to accept the validity and reliability of that promise may be deduced as faith. It is a readiness to believe that what God has promised or stated will occur. On occasions, the Spirit reveals the will of God in situations that may not be referred to in the Bible, be it the identification of a cause of a sickness, the affirmation to undertake a particular action or guidance concerning what one should say or do in a particular situation. On these occasions, the Spirit provides the confidence to support one's actions or words, to be understood as a gift of faith. This does not involve a manufacturing of 'faith' nor is to be equated with natural self-confidence. The faith comes from God and is to be understood as 'assurance' (Heb. 11:1). When God provides a promise, one is assured that it will come to pass and one's faith in the promise is well placed. Similarly, when God supernaturally reveals information for a given situation, the faith to use it is also given by him to accompany that action. He provides faith so that we can partner him in ensuring that his will is accomplished. It aligns us with his purpose, which is always the best.

The statements 'Just have faith' or 'Only believe' are almost meaningless, because faith requires an object. There is nothing mystical in the act of believing. It is not the exercise of faith that brings about the desired change. Faith in itself has no power. The power of faith lies in its object and faith is only as valid as the validity of its object. One does not simply have faith; one has faith in something or someone, in this case, God and his supernatural revelation. Faith does not take up where facts leave off. Faith is not believing something one is not sure of. It is not a leap in the dark but a leap into the light – the light of the revealed word of God, either contained in the Bible or revealed by the Spirit.

Consider the following situation. A man nervously walks on an ice-covered lake. His trepidation is such that he slowly and tentatively tip-toes across the ice, despite the fact that a sign states that the ice is three metres thick. Despite his limited faith, he nevertheless crosses the lake safely, not because he had great confidence, but because the faith that he exercised was based on a reliable fact. If he had believed the sign, he would not have been any more safe in walking on the ice, but he would have known a greater sense of wellbeing as he did so. However, consider another person who presumptuously runs across another ice-covered lake without checking the strength of that which he places his weight upon. If the ice is thin, he will sink whether his 'faith' is great or small. The exercise of faith is less relevant than that on which one's faith is based.

Faith is exercised when one believes what God has said or promised (Rom. 10:17; Eph. 2:8). If God has not said it or promised it, no matter how much 'faith' we manufacture, it will not guarantee the desired result. On those occasions when we have no scriptural guarantee that our prayer will be answered, we should pray according to the knowledge and wisdom that we have at that time. On occasions, God will answer our prayers in the way that we have requested because it was allied to his will. On other occasions, God will provide a gift of faith that will enable us to pray in the assurance that the prayer will be answered in the way that it has been offered. When God gives this kind of faith, we can know that our prayers will be answered before they are actually offered. It is given by God as an assurance that what one is requesting is right. As such, this supernaturally derived confidence or faith does not remain with us constantly. Rather, God reserves it for special occasions when we need it most.

Some time ago, a missionary from Tanzania came to stay with us in our home and in the course of one evening he shared a remarkable story with us that will serve as an example of a gift of faith in operation. He was evangelizing in a remote territory and a crowd of people had gathered to hear his message. In the middle of the talk, a young child cried with alarm as he saw a hungry lioness that had crept towards them. The young missionary realized that it was likely that one of the crowd would be attacked and most probably die. The Bible does not promise protection to believers from such attacks any more than it promises protection from illness. However, as soon as he saw the lioness pacing towards the people, he experienced an unusual desire to instruct the people not to run but to stay as they were. On his instructions, the people responded by remaining motionless.

Very quickly, he realized that this apparently bizarre advice was due to the Spirit's influence, as the lioness was struck by lightning, despite there being clear blue skies. It was discovered afterwards that the animal was injured and would have been likely to have attacked such a group of vulnerable people with little means of protection if the supernatural intervention had not occurred. However, the characteristic of the story of relevance to our discussion is that the missionary concerned had experienced a gift of faith, an assurance that that which he shared with the people was in line with the will of God. Potentially, his advice could have been disastrous if it had not reflected a revelation from God and as such it is a reminder that such activity should not be undertaken lightly. However, it is to be expected that synonymous with such a revelation will be granted a strong sense of assurance that the revelation is authentic.

Some years ago, I prayed for a lady who was to visit a hospital the following day to discuss with a surgeon the removal of a cancerous growth from her body. When I prayed for her, I felt an assurance from God that the operation would not occur because the growth would be miraculously removed. The lady rang me the following evening to confirm the facts as related above – she had been remarkably healed and no surgery was needed. I had prayed for people with cancer before and have subsequently, but this was the only occasion when I experienced this foreknowledge and the sense of assurance that went with it. This gift of faith may be granted in order to allow us to recognize that our prayers are being offered in the will of God or to inform us of our part in fulfilling his designs. However, it is not to be falsely or artificially replicated, nor is it to be pre-sumptuously assumed that this gift can be manipulated or manufactured into being, as great damage can be done to both the confidence of many in God and their perception of God if we act inauthentically.

This gift of faith bears no relationship to the faith needed to see unconditional promises in the Bible coming to pass. The faith needed in those cases is not great: Jesus describing it as big as a 'mustard seed' (Mt. 17:20). That which makes faith effective is the quality of the promise, not faith itself. If God promises something, we only need to believe sufficiently to ask him for it and then to expect it. Some conclusions may be offered:

- If we ask for something that God has already promised, the faith he desires is that we take these promises at face value, believe them and act accordingly.

- If we do not know God's will in a matter, our response should be to pray, trusting him to respond in the best way possible, recognizing that he functions in sovereign authority and limitless power, being motivated by love and wisdom.

- On occasions when we pray, we may feel an assurance that God has heard and is going to answer our prayers in the way that we have requested, even though there are no specific promises along these lines in the Bible. That faith has come from God and may be appro-priately defined as 'a gift of faith'. When this gift is in operation in the context of prayer for another, there is certainty that the sick one being ministered to will be healed.

The confidence undergirding Peter's command that the paralyzed man referred to in Acts 3:1–10 should get up and walk may be identified as being the result of a gift of faith. Why was it that, despite there being many others who would have been lining their route, he was the only one who received their interest? Why was it that they pronounced healing when the man had only asked for money? The answer lies in the fact that they were receptive to any message that the Spirit might want to implant in their minds. Consequently, when they arrived at the place where he lay, they were prompted to pronounce healing because God had already placed in their hearts the knowledge/faith that their request would be granted because that request was in keeping with the will of God. As with Jesus, they listened to God, and when he spoke, they obeyed.

What explanation may be offered concerning those who are identified as suffering illness in Paul's letters?

In Philippians 2:27, Paul comments on the fact that Epaphroditus, described in very positive terms (as Paul's brother and co-worker and Apostle and minister to the Philippians), was ill and had nearly died, though God brought healing to him. Although there is no mention of Paul praying for him, there is little reason to doubt that he did.

However, Paul encourages Timothy (1 Tim. 5:23) to partake of a little wine for the sake of his stomach and frequent illnesses, and records that he left Trophimus sick (2 Tim. 4:20). It is clear that medical therapy (wine) was assumed by Paul to be appropriate for restoration, while suffering in each of the above situations was not viewed as out of the ordinary or something to be kept secret as if it was a sign of failure, lack of faith or unconfessed sin. Although Paul achieved miraculous healings, on these particular occasions he does not refer to any supernatural restorations. It is difficult to draw conclusions from these occurrences but it would be irresponsible to argue that they demonstrate that miraculous healings ceased to occur in the early church or that medicine took on a higher priority for the early believers. The most that may be determined is that illness did not cease as an experience for people once they become Christians.

Paul is aware of the potential benefit of sickness in that it can be a means of chastening. Ananias and Sapphira are disciplined (Acts 5:1ff.) by the most extreme form of sickness: death. Similarly, the church at Corinth was informed that some sickness its members experienced had been caused by sin (1 Cor. 11:30), and Paul recognizes the value of suffering for personal growth (2 Cor. 12:7–10).

What part did sickness/suffering play in Paul's life and ministry?

On some occasions, it is difficult to identify the suffering that is referred to by Paul. However, he does describe his outer nature wasting away (2 Cor. 4:16), which is probably a reference to his perception that his body is dying. In Galatians 4:13, he describes a 'weakness in the flesh', generally understood to be a physical form of suffering, identity uncertain. Because of this weakness, which resulted in his not being able to travel immediately, he remained and consequently preached the Gospel to the Galatians. There is no suggestion that the weakness resulted from personal sin. It may have been assumed that if illness were being referred to, Paul would have referred to it as being in his 'body', rather than in the 'flesh'. However, in response, the term 'weakness' is regularly used of illness. The context of the phrase needs also to be considered. It appears that the weakness restricted Paul from travel, either enforcing his stay in Galatia until his health improved or forcing him into Galatia in the first place. This implies a physical ailment.

It is possible that Paul intended his readers to realize that suffering was a divinely ordained norm for the presentation of the Gospel. For an envoy of a god to be weak or ill was a cultural hurdle to be cleared by the Galatians when they were confronted with Paul; but they achieved it (4:14). At the same time, they had the opportunity to learn an important lesson about God's ways of working in weakness to achieve his purposes.

The description of the condition referred to in Galatians 4:13 provides further guidance in identifying the weakness concerned. The term Paul used to describe how they did not act towards him (*exeptusate*) is often translated 'rejected', but may literally be translated 'spat at' or 'spat out'. This indicates that his condition may have been, if not repulsive, at least a cause of concern or fear to the Galatians. Furthermore, the response by the Galatians to be prepared to give him their eyes (4:15) may indicate that he had an eye disorder, though it may be a metaphor used regardless of one's condition to indicate the quality of their readiness to help him. However, an eye disorder would have been a reason for them to spit at him in order to protect themselves from an 'evil eye'. The reference in Galatians 6:11 concerning the large letters with which Paul writes to the believers is further possible evidence of an eye disorder. Similarly, the statement in the conclusion to 2 Thessalonians (3:17) that Paul writes the greeting with his own hand possibly indicates that this was an unusual incident suggestive of his need of a secretary.

In conclusion, in view of the variety of views expressed, caution is necessary in determining the most appropriate interpretation. Whatever the identity of the weakness referred to, it is clear that Paul was not immune to suffering. Whether he was referring to a specific bodily weakness, such as poor eyesight, or a general form of weakness that accompanied his ministry is not clear. That which is certain is that God chose to demonstrate his grace and power in the context of weakness. A later examination of the identity of his 'thorn in the flesh' may shed some light on the issue. Sufficient to say that God chose to use a form of suffering to extend his Kingdom in Galatia and to achieve his will.

What is the relationship between medicine and other therapies and supernatural healing?

Along with many missionaries in the early twentieth century, Willie Burton, the founder of the Congo Evangelistic Mission, was a missionary who chose not to take quinine, which would have protected him from malaria. He viewed medicine as an inappropriate alternative to trusting in God for supernatural protection, writing 'I would rather die than disgrace His cause.' Others in the CEM also refused and at least nine died as a result. Although few believers would advocate a similar stance today, it is not unknown in some Christian groups similarly to renounce medicine or at least to view it as second best.

Because 2 Chronicles 16:12 condemned King Asa, who preferred to consult the doctors instead of God when he was ill, some have expressed uncertainty about medical therapies. However, the writer is not condemning Asa for recourse to medical practices as such, but because, despite the disease being God's judgement for his lifestyle, he still refused to turn to God for help. Similarly, the negative description of doctors as being 'worthless' in Job 13:4 does not mean that all medical practitioners may be so described. Finally, the fact that the woman with a haemorrhage (Lk. 8:43) spent all her money on medical help for her condition and endured much at the hands of doctors (Mk. 5: 26) is a statement meant to highlight the severity of her condition rather than an indication that medical therapists are inappropriate. Paul actually encouraged Timothy to take advantage of the therapeutic properties of wine, as opposed to water, because of his frequent stomach complaints (1 Tim. 5:23).

It is more appropriate to recognize medical therapy as a gift of God intended to benefit humanity and available alongside supernatural healing. Andrew and Jodie testify to the blessings of the doctors and nurses as well as the supervising and healing nature of God. They experienced both when they were told that the baby they were expecting three months later was doomed to die in the womb. Their church prayed and the medical staff cared. Between them, their son, despite a very perilous first few months, grew into a healthy little boy. Rather than assume that God did it all or that the doctors and nurses achieved all that was needed, they recognized that on this occasion both had played a part in the saving of their son. Although the prognosis was initially bleak, they were grateful for the gifts of medicine and the power of God which had resulted in the healing development of their son.

Increasingly, alternative therapies are being considered as legitimate medical practice and this has resulted in therapies that were once taboo becoming more acceptable to contemporary believers. It is important to be objective but also careful in exploring less-well-known therapies, remembering that many of them have been practiced in some countries for many years. Our worldviews may be the barrier to our considering them, rather than that they represent illegitimate forms of healings. The informed Christian community and the Spirit are the best guides in this respect.

Is it true that more healings occur in non-Western countries and, if so, why?

Because of remarkable records of healings in some countries, it is often assumed that the countries where healings appear to be less common are somehow at fault. It is true that some testimonies of healing occurring in some parts of the world are remarkable and also that, from time to time, some of them are more prominent in some geographical locations than others. A number of explanations for this apparent imbalance may be offered.

- It is possible that that which is needed for healings to occur is more in evidence in some countries and, thus, more healings occur. However, often, such numbers of healings occur in settings where medical aid is very limited. It is to be remembered that the majority of the world does not have ready access to medical aid and prayer for healing is often the only route to restoration available. However, that does not necessarily mean that proportionately more healings occur in those contexts. As believers in the countries concur, disease kills many more than in Westernized areas where medicine is much more accessible. In the former locations, prayer may be offered more regularly because there is no alternative. It may be that there is a greater readiness to ask for God's help, though one must be careful not to assume that everyone who asks for healing, or even a majority who do, are healed. All the major healing evangelists, despite seeing many people healed, acknowledge that a majority remained unhealed. I have many friends in Africa and Asia who acknowledge sickness and suffering is a greater problem among Christians in their communities than it is in Christian communities in more developed countries. Many of these leaders also note that there appears to be little difference in the percentage of those people healed in their countries as compared with other settings. God heals there as he heals in other contexts, but in both, it is his will that determines the outcome.

- It is possible that some believers (who have access to medical aid) have begun to lose sight of the possibility of praying for healing. James 4:2 states 'You have not because you do not ask' and it is possible that some believers have become lethargic in receiving from God that which he may wish to bestow. It may be that they are unaware of these promises, or are too timid or unwilling to ask for a variety of reasons. In 2 Kings 20:1–7, King Hezekiah was told he was to die. In response, he asked the apparently impossible … that God would extend his life. Surprisingly, God acceded to his request and he lived for a further seven years. Sometimes, we may not receive because we do not ask. We have nothing to lose, since God will never give us, by way of response, something that is inappropriate.

- Although some have suggested that a greater expectation for healing has resulted in more healings in some countries, speaking to indigenous church leaders is often helpful. Though many will acknowledge the occurrence of supernatural healings, and many are actively involved in prayer for such, they readily concede that it is too easy to assume that a multiplicity of healings occur in their milieu. Such people provide a wise context in exploring healings that occur elsewhere.

- It is true that some areas of the world where revival is occurring do experience a greater preponderance of healings. This has occurred in revivals in the past and reflects the evangelistic impact of the Gospel in some of the cities in which the Apostles preached, as recorded in the book of Acts.

- Rather than expressing complacency with one's current situation, wherever it is, or cynicism with regard to healing occurrences elsewhere, it is better to seek to be usable by the Spirit whenever restoration is hoped for, wherever one happens to be.

What is the identity and significance of Paul's thorn in the flesh?

Paul refers to this issue in 2 Corinthians 12:7–10, verses which are located in a context (chapters 10–13) where Paul is defending his apostolic status and ministry against his opponents. It is immediately preceded by his description of an inexplicable heavenly experience (12:1–7), as a result of which the thorn was given to him to act as a check on any arrogance he might have felt resulting from this revelation.

The word 'thorn' (*skolops*) is only used here in the NT. Although in classical Greek it was used to refer to a stake on which the head of an enemy was impaled, or used as a defensive measure, by the Christian era it more often described a thorn or splinter. Paul chose not to specify the identity of the thorn and this should act as a caution in one's analysis. What he does reveal is that its presence caused him to pray for its removal, leading instead to a provision of divine strength. Secondly, given his many sufferings recorded in 2 Corinthians 11:23–29, for which it is not recorded that he prayed for their removal, this particular condition must have been severe, given that he prays for its removal three times.

The thorn is described as harassing him, in the present tense (12:7), indicating that it was a continuous or a recurring experience. Meanwhile, the response of the Lord indicates that he would provide ongoing support for the Apostle for this continuing suffering. The impact of the thorn is mentioned twice in the same verse (12:7), described by Paul as intended to keep him from being too elated, whilst at the same time providing him with an opportunity to receive support from God. One way the thorn achieved its objective was to remind Paul of his own weakness and inability to succeed without the support of God. At the same time, it provided an ongoing reminder that God chooses to work best in the context of weakness, best seen in the cross, and referred to by Paul as such in 1 Corinthians 1:18–31.

Paul attributes the affliction to an angel/messenger of Satan. Two explanations are available:

(i)   God allowed Satan to affect Paul with the thorn, resulting in Satan accomplishing God's will, or
(ii) Satan unilaterally, and of his own volition, enforced the thorn on Paul.

While the latter provides Satan with the authority that he might dream about but never own, the former option provides the more likely rationale. Although Satan may have intended to wreak havoc and obstruct Paul's ministry, he is but a pawn in the grand design, and God, who is the supreme guide of all events, instead uses the thorn for the benefit and development of Paul whilst also revealing his capacity and willingness to support him. This does not mean that suffering per se always provides opportunities for God's will to be accomplished, though often valuable lessons may be learned through suffering.

Interpretations as to the identity of the thorn have varied. Three main options are available:

(i) *Opposition.* The thorn has been identified with persecution. In support of this view, it has been noted that the OT uses the metaphor of a thorn to describe opposition from people (Num. 33:55; Josh. 23:13), and 2 Corinthians is a defence against Paul's opposers.

   Although one wonders whether Paul would ever pray for the removal of his enemies, elsewhere (Rom. 15:31; 2 Thes. 3:2) he did. Finally, the reference to the angel of Satan in 12:7 is preceded by references to servants of Satan (i.e. Paul's opponents) in 11:15, while the phrase 'I beat with a fist' (12:7) links more directly to the idea of people.

(ii) *Illness.* The fact that the thorn is described as being 'in the flesh' is suggestive, though not conclusive, of it being a physical illness. The involvement of Satan in illness is located in the OT (Job 2:5) and the NT (Lk. 13:16) and Paul may be referring to an illness such as malaria or an eye disorder.

(iii) *Pressures associated with his ministry.* It is possible that Paul is referring to the suffering that he experienced because of his apostolic mission and status, as described in 11:25–27 and as prophesied in Acts 9:16. As Jesus experienced spiritual torment in Gethsemane and initially prayed for its removal, so also Paul may have prayed for the removal of this burden until he had been assured that God would support him.

Whatever the identity of the thorn, the important elements for the readers relate to its value as a means of guarding Paul from pride and the fact that it was to be accompanied by God's grace that would ensure he could live with it. The description of his suffering referred to in 1 Corinthians 12:10 provides extra evidence that Paul is prepared to describe his sufferings as the valid vehicle for the achieving of the will of God in his life. That he refers to the death of Jesus in 1 Corinthians 13:4 as being in weakness more closely identifies the role of suffering with weakness. However, the crux of the issue is that it is in suffering that the grace and power of God is made perfect. Because of this potential of victory being achieved through suffering, Paul refrains from praying further for its removal.

Implications for the Contemporary Church

Healing is not discussed by Paul to any great degree. It occurs, in the main, in response to questions raised by believers, though not in relation to the topics of sickness/ healing. He offers no systematic presentation or guidelines concerning healing; to a large degree he ignores the issue of exorcism and explores the concept of suffering instead.

This, in itself, provides a valuable perspective when seeking information on the topic of healing from the Pauline literature. It is of considerably less significance to Paul than are other issues affecting believers. For Paul, it appears that although signs and wonders were normative for his mission activity, the supernatural wellbeing of believers was a greater priority than their physical health. Wholeness in their relationship with God and each other were the areas that he emphasized in his teaching while issues of health were viewed in the context of a life to come that would provide physical restoration for all believers.

That is not to say that physical restoration was of minimal importance to Paul. Rather, other characteristics relating to life and spirituality were his priorities. As far as healing was concerned, he preferred to identify the Spirit as the one who retained the responsibility for such activity, through believers. Thus, Paul regularly emphasized the importance of believers being led by the Spirit in their relationship with each other so that they could benefit from his wisdom and healing power when appropriate.

A number of comments may be offered concerning the information provided by Paul concerning this topic:

- God affirmed Paul through the healings that accompanied his ministry. They reflected the ministry of healing as achieved by Jesus.

- Believers should be encouraged to follow the leading of the Spirit with regard to the implementation of healing.

- In his letters, Paul comments less on healing. That is not to say that healings ceased to occur. However, it is of significance to note that he writes more about suffering than he does about restoration from it or its removal. Instead, he speaks about its presence in the life of a believer as being normative, a point echoed elsewhere in the NT (Jas. 1:2,3,12, 5:10,11; 1 Pet. 1:6, 2:19–25, 4:4,12–19).

- Although not all suffering is intended to provide lessons for suffering believers and those around them, the testimony of Paul (2 Cor. 12) should at least encourage us to consider such a possibility. If this is so, it is to be assumed that God will make this clear. Without such revelation from God, it is unnecessary to assume that the suffering has been provided to reveal the presence of sin.

- The presence of God in the life of the suffering believer is a powerful truth that should be encountered, explored and applied.

- Paul's writings concerning gifts of healing were offered in the broader context of establishing guidelines concerning the importance of the fact that the readers were to recognize that, as a body of believers, they were interdependent (1 Cor. 12). He chose to concentrate on the latter while offering no explanation concerning the administration of gifts of healings. The book of Acts provides information concerning his healing ministry, but Paul does not offer a developed framework of healing for the members of his churches, with very little information concerning its praxis.

- It is possible that Paul anticipated that healing was, to a large degree, an apostolic ministry, and not appropriate as a function of the majority of believers. However, the references in 1 Corinthians are obstacles to such a view as well as the fact that he chose to concentrate on other issues of more importance to his readers, such as doctrinal matters or ethical behaviour, rather than healing praxis.

- There is, however, a distinction to be drawn between the ministry of Paul and that of Jesus in that while Paul viewed suffering, including illness, as having a chastening benefit as well as being part of the lot for the believer (and the unbeliever), Jesus never countenanced the possibility of sickness being of value, always choosing to remove it from those who came to him for restoration.

- James 5:13–18 provides guidance for healing in the context of a Christian community and, as such, complements the information offered by Paul.

6. Healing in James

Introduction

The book of James is important for studying the topic of healing. Not only is it one of the earliest books in the NT, but it was also written by the leader of the most important Christian centre in the early church, based in Jerusalem. Chapter 5:13–18 provide a practical framework for healing that is also applicable to healing situations today. Given the above, and the unfortunate fact that the early church infrequently applied the advice, it is instructive to consider the salutary suggestions presented by James.

Much exposition of this passage has tended to polarize its teaching. Either the author is seen to be promulgating medical therapy or a spiritual ministry, a restoration to physical health or spiritual wellbeing. Instead, it will be proposed that James is advocating the re-establishment of wholeness in a context of pastoral concern in the Christian community, in which spiritual and physical harmony is to be maintained as a result of prayer, forgiveness and righteous lifestyles.

The verses concerned connect the wisdom of God with faith and practice in the context of suffering; all are prominent themes in the epistle as a whole. As such, this passage (5:13–18) provides an important final context for dominant themes of the epistle, which are also reflected in the first passage (1:1–12). Both passages are set in contexts of suffering; both concentrate on the central themes of wisdom and prayer offered in faith, and both comment on the response of God to the one suffering. Therefore, rather than seeing 5:13–18 as part of a less significant conclusion, left to the end because of its relative unimportance, it is preferable to see the passage and the practice contained therein as an integral part of the whole teaching of the letter. In it, James provides his readers with an opportunity to incorporate the significant features of his message in a practical ministry to those suffering, encapsulating mutual concern and a recognition of the need for wisdom from God.

Although little information is provided in the letter to identify the author (1:1), it has generally been accepted that it consists of information provided by James, the brother of Jesus. As one of the most important leaders, the one who chaired the Council of Jerusalem (Acts 15) and who was described as a pillar in the church by Paul (Gal. 2:9), the author of this letter speaks from a prestigious position. As such, the book forms a very early and important insight into the thinking of the church concerning healing.

James's Jewish background is of importance in clarifying some of his detailed guidelines that would otherwise be lost to a non-Jewish audience. The Jewish flavour of the contents (2:2, 5:4), especially the OT quotations (1:10,11, 2:8,11,23, 4:6) and allusions (1:10, 2:21,23,25, 3:9, 5:2,11,17,18), the stress on the Jewish Law (2:9–11, 4:11,12), the mention of the Jewish fundamental concept of the unity of God (2:19), the use of OT examples (Elijah, Rahab, Job, Abraham, Isaac) and the freedom in using Jewish terms (apparently without any consideration for any potential Gentile readers), all suggest a Jewish–Christian authorship and readership. As a result of this brief exploration of the author, it is possible to deduce that 5:13–18:

- provide an insight into the healing practice of the first Christian–Jewish community;
- consist of advice offered by one of the most important leaders in the church;
- are best understood when their Jewish context is borne in mind;
- describe a church-based context for healing.

James offers his guidelines in a deliberately comprehensive way to accommodate a wide scenario of ministry opportunities, offering a path to wholeness and healing in their fullest sense – a potential harmony of the physical, emotional, mental and spiritual aspects of a person. James is not only offering hope for those in his community who are physically ill, but also for those who find themselves marginalized as a result of other forms of weakness.

Significant Questions

Who may receive prayer?

All modern translations of James 5:14–18 refer to the identity of the suffering concerned as being sickness. As a result of this, most readers have assumed that the ministry offered in the passage is only relevant for those who are (seriously) physically ill. But are they right? As we will see, the fundamental meaning of the words used is 'weakness', not 'sickness'.

Does one have to be physically ill to receive prayer from the elders as referred to by James?
David had never been ill in his life, not really ill. But on that Friday, he felt worse than he'd ever felt before. It started when he opened the letter that was delivered in the mail and that was now discarded, rolled up in a crumpled ball in the corner of the room. He managed to get through the first few hours in the office, though achieved very little. His friends could tell there was something wrong, though he wasn't ill. Throughout the day, despair flooded his soul, and hope fled. As a new Christian, he knew that God could help and, by chance, he turned to James 5:14–18 and read about the elders praying for people who were sick. However, although he had never felt weaker in his life, he wasn't sick, and so he endured his darkest night alone without the aid of others.

Sickness is not the only cause of one being marginalized or disabled. Other forms of weakness lead to one being destabilized or lacking in wholeness that can, on occasions, be even more incapacitating than physical illness. Stress, discouragement, spiritual weakness, emotional weariness and fear are some examples of conditions that are not normally defined as sickness but which can be as debilitating and as damaging, if not more so, than some forms of physical sickness to the individual concerned. On the surface, however, it would appear that such sufferers are not able to benefit from the ministry of the elders as outlined by James.

However, it is probable that James's instructions have been too narrowly interpreted, thus ruling out areas of weakness that may also be identified as valid causes for prayer by a church leadership. The variety of words used by the author to refer to the weakness concerned indicates that while physical illness is not to be ruled out as a form of weakness that may warrant the prayer of the elders, other types of weakness may also be envisaged.

A form of weakness that may be excluded from the guidelines in 5:14–18 is that caused by persecution, including the normal sufferings that sometimes co-exist with being a Christian. In 5:13, James refers to the value of prayer being offered in times of suffering. The word translated as 'suffering' (*kakopatheō*) in 5:13 is also located in 5:10, where it describes the experience of the OT prophets. In the OT, the prophets are rarely described as being ill, but are often identified as suffering as a result of their being the representatives of God, often including persecution. In 5:13, James uses the same word of believers, referring to the difficult experiences that often result from living as a Christian in a secular world. Such sufferings are not necessarily removed, though prayer is advocated as a means of gaining strength to bear them. However, 5:14–18 refer to other sufferings and, to make this clear, James uses two different words to describe them.

Sickness or weakness?

There are two Greek terms normally translated 'sick' in this passage in most bibles. However, elsewhere, both of them are used in many different settings to identify a much wider range of differing forms of weakness. To restrict their translation to forms of illness may be premature.

The term 'sick', used in verse 14, is a translation of the Greek verb *astheneō*. The fundamental meaning of this word is 'weakness' and the presence of the first letter of the word, '*a*', identifies it as being the opposite of the word for 'strength' (*shenēs*). The term 'weakness' (*astheneia*) is used in Jewish, Christian and secular Greek writings of that era to refer to a variety of conditions, including spiritual weakness, physical weakness, weariness and sickness. The most that may be determined concerning its translation in James 5:14 is that it may refer to any or all of the above options. At this stage, it would be incautious to designate 'sickness' as the only or even main translation of *astheneō*. Rather, it is possible that *astheneō* was intended by the author to indicate a wide range of conditions of weakness.

The second word that is generally translated as 'sick' (5:15) is the Greek *kamnō*, which may also be translated in a variety of ways. It is only used once elsewhere in the NT (Heb. 12:3), where it refers to weariness. A meaning akin to general physical weariness would seem to be closest to the historical understanding of the term. This, of course, does not exclude the possibility of it being used to mean sickness or a weariness caused by sickness, but neither should it necessarily be only used to indicate sickness. The context, not the term itself, helps to determine the precise interpretation and the most that may be stated of the guidelines offered by James is that he is anticipating ministry to those in the Christian community who are marginalized as a result of some weakness they are experiencing. In that respect, it seems wisest to retain the widest possible option of interpretation unless proof to the contrary is presented.

Similarly, the terms used to describe the restoration process, namely 'save' (5:15), 'raise' (5:15) and 'heal' (5:16), are also used with a variety of meanings dependent on the context. It is apparent that all the terms are appropriate to scenarios of physical illness, though other conditions of weakness are not to be excluded as settings for their use also.

When the word 'save' (*sōzō*) is used elsewhere in the book of James (1:21, 2:14, 4:12, 5:20), the author is referring to the hope of spiritual salvation. Its inclusion in 5:15 needs to be considered against this background. It is quite possible that *sōzō* in James 5:15 also refers to spiritual salvation. This has been its central use in the other references in the letter. However, the immediate context of the word is of importance in determining its meaning as well as its usage elsewhere. What is clear is that elsewhere in the NT and beyond, the term is capable of a variety of different meanings, including 'preserve from danger', 'rescue', 'protect', the contexts relating to physical and spiritual settings as well as healing of sickness. In other words, the identity of the salvation is determined by the situation from which the sufferer is rescued; for James, this may be broader than has been hitherto assumed by many.

The term 'raise' (5:15) is a translation of a Greek word (*egeirō*) that also has a variety of meanings dependent on the context. If the situation of the sufferer is one of sickness, it could describe his or her being raised, either physically or metaphorically. If the person is spiritually discouraged or physically or emotionally weary, the meaning would relate to him or her being metaphorically raised from that position of weakness.

The final term under consideration (*iaomai*) is generally translated as 'heal' (5:16), but again, this word is capable of a number of translations, depending on the context of its use. It is used to refer to physical healing but also of healing of relationships or the forgiveness of sins, the latter having particular significance in the preceding context where James refers to the importance of praying for one another in the context of confession.

It is probable that James is being deliberately all encompassing in his presentation of the healing ministry

of the church in order that the promise of God to the
sufferer may be seen to involve physical and spiritual
benefits. For those needing spiritual or physical
restoration, or both, the path to recovery is revealed by
James to be by prayer for one another. Rather than restrict
the healing process to sickness only, it is more
appropriate to anticipate that James is expecting a wider
range of weaknesses to be ministered to by the local
church.

Application
- It is probable that James anticipates the possibility of a
  wide form of healing, depending on the suffering
  concerned. It has already been noted that the key
  words referred to are capable of receiving a number of
  interpretations. Although these include contexts of
  physical healing of sicknesses, other scenarios need
  not be excluded.

- James evades a dogmatic route and instead chooses to
  be comprehensive to provide the possibility of wider
  benefits to sufferers, offering a path to wholeness and
  healing in their fullest sense, a harmony of the
  physical, emotional, mental and spiritual aspects of a
  person. Thus, James is not only offering hope for those
  in his community who are physically ill, but also for
  those who find themselves marginalized and disabled
  as a result of weakness in their lives.

- James is best understood as offering pastoral
  guidance that encompasses a comprehensive range of
  weaknesses and/or illnesses for which prayer may be
  offered. While this should not exclude sickness,
  neither should it exclude life-changing experiences
  that are not identified with sickness. For all believers
  who are feeling weak or weary, for a range of reasons,

the role of the leaders is to pray for them in order that they be strengthened and restored to fellowship with their Christian community.

• The role of the church is to develop wholeness in its members and this may be achieved in relation to a number of forms of weakness. Prayer and ministry should thus be offered for many different varieties of weakness experienced by believers, including, but not only involving, sickness.

Who is encouraged to pray for those needing restoration?

James recommends that the first action by those suffering should be to call for the elders, who are to take particular responsibility in praying for those who are in need. That is not to say that they should be the only ones who should pray; in verse 16 he encourages others to be involved.

Although used to describe old(er) people in Jewish literature, the term 'elder' is also used to designate leaders who formed the ruling councils of cities and tribes (Gen. 50:7; Lev. 4:15; Judg. 8:14,16). In the NT, elders are identified as leaders of local churches (Acts 11:30, 14:23, 15:2). That which may be concluded concerning the elders referred to in James is that they were probably Christian leaders who, because of their age or office or both, functioned in a way that best suited them for wise pastoral ministry.

The corporate activity of elders is central to the pattern advocated by James; they act together, rather than individually. The significance of their being summoned may also be linked to their representative nature. It is probable that they were from the same community as the ones needing prayer, their desire being to remind sufferers of their permanent and important place within the community despite any temporary absence and, most importantly, to pray for them. The fact that they, as leaders of the community, visited them demonstrated the sense of loss that they felt at their absence and the importance of the one who was suffering.

The significance of the role of the elder is further appreciated when the righteousness of the person offering prayer is explored (5:16). Two questions need to be answered concerning this issue. To whom is James referring (or, to put it differently, what/who is a righteous prayer/person) and why is the prayer of such a person so significant?

It is possible that James is using the term 'righteous' to describe a Christian, thus indicating that all believers may so pray effectively; this is how the term is sometimes used by Paul (Rom. 5:19). However, given the Jewish background of James, it is more likely that he is using the term 'righteous' to describe those believers whose lives are particularly upright. In Jewish society, the righteous person was identified by his/her moral lifestyle in relationship to God and his/her community. Such people were identified by their awe of God (Ex. 18:21), their piety and love for God (Job 15:14) and their willingness to serve God and others (Ps. 37:21). In the time of James, such people were described as being trustworthy and fruitful, living in accordance with the Scriptures.

That the righteous person is specified by James as the person whose prayers are powerful is due to his/her relationship with God. This characteristic of active righteousness is integral to James's perception of righteousness, in itself, central to the letter (2:21–25, 3:18, 5:6). Similarly, throughout the NT, the term is used as a contrast to disobedience, being descriptive of good behaviour (Mt. 5:45; Lk. 1:17; Acts 24:15; Rom. 3:10). This righteous lifestyle is integrally linked with an ongoing relationship with God and is used not as a description of status but as a definition of character, lifestyle and attitude. The righteous person, identified by James, is able to offer effective prayers because he or she will pray in accordance with God's will. The believer who tries to keep God's laws is unlikely to pray in an unacceptable manner. Rather, such a person will seek God's will for the occasion. Thus, the prayer of a righteous person is powerful, not because the prayer is accepted by God because of the meritorious nature of the one praying, but because that person is able, because of a close relationship with God, to discern how best to pray.

Application
- Since few churches follow the Jewish–Christian leadership model anticipated by James, equivalent leaders to the NT elders should undertake this responsibility. It is incumbent on people entrusted with this role that they be actively committed to the principles of Christian conduct.

- In supporting a believer who is suffering, it is preferable that a number of believers visit and pray, thus demonstrating the importance of the one who is absent from the fellowship whilst also offering a context of mutual support in the process of prayer and seeking of God's will.

- Prayer for those who are suffering should be undertaken in the expectation that God will provide wisdom concerning how to pray. Whilst one ear should be attuned to the person receiving prayer, the other should be available to the wisdom and guidance offered by God.

What is the significance of the prayer of faith?

The feature of prayer is integral to this passage, being mentioned eight times in just six verses, and is the determining factor in the healing process. The prayer of faith (5:15), only used here in the NT, and the significance of faith in a healing scenario have been a cause of confusion to many, often resulting in guilt on the part of those whose situation has not changed after prayer. James clearly expects the prayer of faith to succeed. In the absence of such success, many suggestions have been offered, often related to insufficient faith or the presence of unconfessed sin on the part of the sufferer.

It is possible that 5:15 finds its closest parallel in 1:6 (and possibly 2:23) inasmuch as the shared context is a prayer of request. The faith that is anticipated in 1:6 (2:23) is trust in God's promise, on the basis of which one is encouraged to pray and expect a positive response. It is in this respect that faith in 5:15 is most appropriately interpreted. The faith needed in 5:15 is to be understood as trust that God will do as he has promised or desires rather than trust that God will do as we ask. The difficulty with the latter alternative is that it presents prayer as the master of God, makes faith meritorious and provides little guidance for those situations that do not result in restoration after prayer.

The relationship between prayer and faith in 1:6 is dependent on the knowledge that God is able and willing to provide that which he has promised, namely wisdom. Similarly, the faith reflected in 2:23 is to be defined as a belief that God will honour his promises and fulfil his revealed will. This is to be recognized also in the context of 5:15. James thus encourages his readers to pray according to the will of God and to accompany this with acts that reflect God's desire.

The significance of prayer is not just to inform God of particular needs, but also to give the supplicant the opportunity to discover the most appropriate way to pray, recognizing that God knows best. To desire God's will in prayer is a positive aim. As Jewish tradition involved the hope that prayer offered should be in the will of God, so also prayer in James 5:15 is offered in the same belief that God's will should be sought in prayer.

In the context of 5:15, the relationship between the sufferer and God must be developed to bring about interaction and absorption of the former into the will of the latter. The characteristic, which brings faith into existence, is the will of God. The prayer of faith can only thus be offered if the will of God is in keeping with the prayer. It is only in this context that James can offer a guarantee of restoration.

What is faith?

Some suggest that supernatural healing is promised to all believers and faith is to be equated with the belief that healing is the guaranteed right of the believer. Thus, it is suggested that before God will heal, one has to believe that he is going to do so. Anything less than this is deemed to result in rejection by God as far as receiving healing is concerned. The fear that a lack of faith has obstructed God in his desire to heal has resulted in many experiencing guilt due to an unnecessary perception that one may have been a block to one's own healing or that of another.

Nevertheless, the phenomenon of claiming one's healing has been popularized, further encouragement being offered that the prayer should not include the phrase 'if it be your will' but 'according to your will'. Similarly, some have taught that prayer should result in believing that we have already received the answer to our prayer, even though the sickness remains and even when there is no sign of improvement.

Furthermore, others have taught that one should not allow oneself to think of one's sickness, as such thoughts are viewed as being harmful to one's potential healing. Rather than hope for healing, one is exhorted to believe that it has already occurred, and symptoms of illness are to be identified as fictitious experiences or lies of the devil imposed on the body to make one think that the healing has not occurred.

These perspectives are not supported in the healing ministry of Jesus. Jesus does not condemn doubt nor demand faith; there is no evidence of symptoms remaining after the healing; neither is it recorded that ongoing symptoms are a test of one's faith, nor does Jesus request gratitude before the healing occurs. At the same time, biblical support for God subjecting people to such treatment to prove their faith concerning an apparent promise of healing is lacking. Our integrity is maintained by acknowledging our problems, not pretending that they do not exist, and it is unhelpful to live as if one's suffering is not real.

The faith that is often demanded by some in such situations is based on the apparently unconditional promises contained in the NT (Mt. 21:22; Mk 11:24; Jn. 14:14) and consists of a belief that God's will is unreservedly committed to healing in this life. An absence of restoration following prayer for the sufferer is often interpreted as being due to a lack of faith, thus constituting doubt in what is perceived to be a promise of God. However, a lack of faith, as presented in the NT, is not to be identified with an uncertainty as to whether God will heal or not, but with a rejection of him and his claims to heal. Furthermore, evidence that God has provided an unconditional guarantee of healing in this life is not reflected in the Bible. Therefore, to claim it is an act of presumption.

Another popular view concerning faith is based on the belief that it can be increased. Thus, one is recommended to start praying for lesser ailments before one prays for more severe problems. The implication of this thinking is that one's confidence grows the more success one experiences. However, this unhelpfully places the onus on the person offering the prayer rather than God who answers the prayer. Such descriptions of faith find little support in the NT. The faith anticipated by James is not measured quantitatively, on the basis of the assumption that the more one has, the more likely restoration will occur.

Many of the responses to an absence of healing are problematic, often insensitive and largely unsupported by biblical evidence. In general, the answers provided for the many cases of unfulfilled healing are such that the initial theory of unconditional healing for all believers must be questioned, for it appears to present an arbitrary characteristic in God. The relevant key verses must always be interpreted in a wider context, which includes a recognition of the importance of the will of God, for there are significant problems in attempting to substantiate a theory that God unconditionally promises to all believers comprehensive healing and restoration to wholeness. An attendant danger for some is that suffering is viewed as an alien experience for believers and those suffering are assumed to be people who are somehow outside normative Christian experience. A greater awareness of the potential role of suffering in the development of the life of the believer as reflected in the Bible and the lives of Christians through the centuries is important.

If the promise for supernatural healing is conditional, depending instead on each particular situation and God's perfect response to it, the problems associated with an absence of healing are significantly lessened. Faith is not then regarded as a package that is presented to God in response to which he must accede, irrespective of his better judgement. In addition, the apparent failures in healing may not be thrust back upon the sufferer as further burdens of guilt and anxiety, but are to be interpreted, at times, as God's perfect plan for those concerned. At other times, God may choose to deliver believers from their particular condition of suffering. What must at all times be maintained is the recognition that to know his will and seek to pray within it is at the heart of the recommendation offered by James.

Application
- The faith expressed by those who came to Jesus in his earthly ministry and those who are instructed to call for the elders is anticipated as being the same. They are coming to God (via Jesus or the elders) in the belief that he can meet their need. While Jesus healed all, and in so doing confirmed his unique mission, the contemporary sufferer is responded to according to the perfect will of God, which might result in restoration. Undergirding both the ministry of Jesus and that of the elders is the will of God, though that need not be the same in both settings.

- The prayer of faith appears to be identical to the gift of faith as described by Paul (1 Cor. 12:9). The gift of faith is to be understood as a gift given by the Spirit on certain occasions, to be identified as knowledge of God's will for that particular situation when no scriptural guidance is available. Resulting from such divinely imparted knowledge, an individual may confidently expect that the outcome, as revealed, will occur. Such a gift comes because of a revelation received from God (Rom. 10:17). Consequently, when prayer is offered, an attempt should be made to ascertain the will of God in order to pray most appropriately (1:6). In this context, the leaders (5:14) and/or the righteous person (5:16), because of their experience, wisdom and righteous lifestyles, are best suited to offer such a prayer. Such a prayer is to be offered by one who has taken time to tap God's resource of wisdom and appropriate it to a particular situation. Only this prayer can provide the comprehensive guarantee of restoration promised by James.

- Some practical guidelines for the potential development of this capacity in the life of a believer may be advanced, although it is remembered that all such guidance is to be offered in the context that all the gifts available to the church are ultimately distributed by the Spirit and are subject to his sovereignty (1 Cor. 12:4–11). Nevertheless, the following are of value:
  (i) A development of one's relationship with God through prayer and the reading of Scripture will lead to a greater appreciation of the mind of God and a deeper knowledge of Christ.
  (ii) A developing awareness of the presence of the Spirit in one's life can lead to a greater expectation that his resources, made available to all believers, may be directly used in a given situation in which one may be a channel of God's power for the benefit of others.

(iii)   A readiness to request that God would provide a
        gift of faith in a situation where it is needed is
        an appropriate measure when prayer is being
        offered.

(iv)   In the absence of a certainty that restoration will
        occur, prayer should still be offered. One's role in
        this is to present the sufferer before the Lord. It is
        his responsibility to decide the outcome. What-
        ever occurs, one can be certain that in bringing
        the person to the Lord a positive impact is to be
        expected. He responds out of love and wisdom.
        This is far from a fatalistic approach as the Lord is
        the one who carefully charts our lives with our
        eternal destiny in mind.

(v)   The need to recognize the importance of this gift
        is fundamentally a recognition of one's depen-
        dency on God. The moment that pride begins to
        motivate the desire to receive the gift of faith is
        the time to reconsider one's participation in this
        ministry.

*Why does James state that people should be anointed with
oil?*

Jesus did not anoint people with oil, though he recommended that his disciples did so (Mk. 6:13). The reference
to anointing with oil in James may be related to that
instruction, though it is by no means certain. Anointing
the sick with oil is not recorded in the healing narratives
in Acts. There are two main suggestions for the recommendation of the use of oil by James. The first is that it
may be due to its medical properties, the other because of
its symbolic value.

Medicine
The OT (2 Chr. 28:15; Is. 1:6; Jer. 8:22) refers to the
medicinal properties of oil, though the term 'anoint'

(*aleiphō*, used in James 5:14, is never used in a medicinal context in the OT, nor is there any Jewish evidence that oil was administered in the context of prayer. Nevertheless, Josephus records that doctors recommended Herod, in his final illness, bathe in oil, and Philo praises the medicinal properties of oil, especially in the toning of muscles. It was also regarded as being a medicinal agent outside Judaism, Seneca referring to the benefit of anointing for seasickness. Similarly, Pliny and Galen recommend the medicinal application of oil, Galen noting its use in cases of paralysis, while Pliny declares its usefulness in combating toothache. Celsus states that oil was used to treat many diseases, though he carefully qualifies this statement. Therefore, because of the well-known medicinal properties of oil in Jewish and non-Jewish societies, it is possible that this is reflected in James 5.

However, although the therapeutic value of oil was accepted in the era under consideration, there are difficulties if the sole, or even main, use of oil in James's guidelines involved its medical properties. It is unclear, for example, why its administration is restricted to the elders by James. Another major obstacle to the view that James anticipated a medical use of oil is that it pre-supposes that 5:14–16 reflect only a scenario of sickness. Although this may have been one of the forms of suffering anticipated by James, it is inappropriate to assume that it was the only one and the exploration of the passage concerned thus far substantiates the probability of a wider arena of weakness and suffering.

Perhaps more importantly, although the medical properties of oil were well known at that time, they were only ever expected to alleviate suffering in a limited range of illnesses. There are thus serious deficiencies in assigning this as the only reason for the inclusion of anointing by James. It is necessary to consider other

possible uses of oil in Jewish society that may provide a
more appropriate frame of reference for its use in James 5.

Symbolic properties
Oil was regarded by the Jews as symbolizing a number of
characteristics that would encourage the one who was
being anointed. As such, it indicated the presence of the
Spirit (1 Sam. 10:1,6, 16:13) and was used to signify an
infusion of God's strength (Ps. 89:20–25) or wisdom (Is.
11:2). Anointing was also associated with restoration,
occurring when a person had been healed of leprosy,
such an act proving his or her purification (Lev.
14:12–16), based on which he or she was welcomed back
into society. On other occasions, oil was used to
demonstrate that a new situation had come into being
(including the completion of a marriage or business
contract and the legitimate emancipation of a slave). This
aspect would have been most encouraging to those about
to be anointed, for it would articulate within them a hope
that their suffering would soon be over. Anointing was
also linked with joy (Ps. 45:7), abstention from oil
signifying a time of mourning (2 Sam. 12:20). Thus, James
includes a symbol of joy in association with prayer for
one who is suffering. Although this appears initially to be
incongruous, it is clarified by the expectation of
restoration that he offers.

Anointing with oil was also linked with friendship
and love (Ps. 23:5, 133:2) as well as being understood as
being a gift of God (Jer. 31:12). It was also associated with
the bestowal of honour and affirmation (Mt. 26:7; Lk.
7:46) and, since it was regarded as being precious, the one
who was anointed was also deemed to be special.

The Jews also used oil as part of religious formulae, the
anointing with oil authorizing a separation by God of
prophets (1 Sam. 10:1, 16:1) and priests (Lev. 8:12) for his

service. Not only does this imply the importance to God of those anointed, but it also suggests the idea that God will care for them (Ps. 84:9). Such a thought would be highly suggestive to sufferers in James's Christian–Jewish community. If the anointing procedure transmitted only some of these implications, it is clear why he included it in his advice.

The anointing with oil is thus probably intended to be symbolic and commemorative of certain features that would result in the sufferer feeling secure, knowing that he or she was in the presence of friends who cared and a God who restored. This symbolic usage of anointing finds a ready and comprehensive reservoir of information in the OT, for although anointing is not related to healing situations there, the religious and symbolic connotations are manifest.

Application
- Inasmuch as James's addressees are Jewish Christians, and because he does not explain the practice, it may be assumed that, at least in part, it derived from their Jewish culture. It is probable that the author desires to link the therapeutic properties of oil with the symbolic characteristics to offer a wide-ranging hope to sufferers, the symbolism of the oil providing the most appropriate lens through which the use of oil in James 5:14 is to be examined. Through its use, James offers hope to all who are weak, whether they are physically sick, emotionally distressed or spiritually discouraged.

- Believers are to be encouraged to fulfil the pastoral objectives of James in his use of oil and the symbolic value of oil should be explained. It may be possible to adopt a culturally acceptable alternative, such as a gift of some sort, that would represent some of the symbolic properties of oil for the benefit of the one being prayed for in order to act as an adjunctive support to the use of oil.

What is the importance of the use of the name of the Lord in prayer?

James encourages the readers to employ the name of the Lord in their prayers. The term 'the name' is employed on eight occasions in the NT (excluding James 5:14) relating to healings/exorcisms, of which six refer to exorcisms (Mt. 7:22; Mk. 9:38; Lk. 9:49,50, 10:17–20; Acts 16:18, 19:13) and two to healings (Acts 3:6, 9:34). Three main conclusions may be drawn concerning the significance of the use of the name (of the Lord) in prayer.

The name is associated with power and authority
In the NT, the name of the Lord is used as a representation of his authority, this feature being present elsewhere (1 Sam. 17:45; Acts 3:6). Indeed, the 'name' of the Lord and the 'power' of the Lord often appear to be used synonymously in the Bible (2 Kgs. 2:24; Acts 3:16), and the incorporation of the name of the Lord by James undergirds an expectation to experience his power.

The legitimate and authoritative use of the name necessitates a relationship with the name bearer
Acts 19:13–16 record an incident in which Jewish exorcists attempted an exorcism using the name of the Lord Jesus. Although they assumed a residential power associated with the name, the ineffective nature of the exorcism reveals that such power is not released unconditionally. Although the exorcists knew the name of Jesus, they had no claim to his authority. Their use of the name was illegitimate since there was no relationship

existing with the name bearer. Without authorization, the name itself was powerless, resulting in their powerlessness. Similarly, Matthew 7:21–23 records that knowledge of the name of Jesus does not guarantee relationship with Jesus. However, if one is experiencing a relationship with the Lord, it is a privilege to be able to use his name in prayer, recognizing who he is and realizing that he has granted us the benefit of accessing his resources.

The valid and effective use of the name occurs when the will of the name bearer is invoked
The phrase 'in the name of the Lord' in James 5:14 is the only occasion where it is used in the context of a prayer for restoration. Its meaning is therefore to be carefully defined and its appropriate use determined. Its most proximate occurrence is 5:10, where it refers to prophets who spoke with the authority of the Lord or, more generally, on behalf of the Lord. The words they spoke were not their own but were initiated by God and thus in keeping with his will.

In the context of prayer, the activation of the authority to restore is based on adherence to his will (Jas. 1:25; 1 Jn. 5:14,15). Thus, to pray in the name of Jesus is equivalent to praying that his will would be done; it is to offer the prayer that he would pray. The name of the Lord is therefore appropriately used when the prayer incorporating it is sanctioned or commissioned by God, for then it will effect a change.

Application
- It is possible that the phrase 'in the name of the Lord' is employed simply to designate the identity of the one who is hearing the prayer. However, it is probable that the phrase is included because of its association with the power and, more importantly, the will of the

Lord. Thus, it is to be expected that the sovereign authority of the name bearer will be directed to the sufferer.

• The legitimate presentation of the name necessitates a relationship with the name bearer and assumes a context that is in keeping with the identification of the will of God, because of which he will grant the release of his power to effect the desired transformation.

• To use the name of the Lord appropriately in prayer means that the one praying should seek to hear from God as to how and what to pray. All our requests are like cheques dispatched to heaven that will be validated if they receive his signature. The role of the believer is to ask, the role of the Lord is to respond, the believer also being encouraged to seek to identify his will in the process. This means that if the healing does not occur, rather than simply continue to offer the same request, more pertinent counsel could be offered and more time spent listening to God should be encouraged.

What is the relationship between sin, forgiveness and healing?

James indicates that, on occasions, suffering might be related to personal sin, a belief echoed in Paul. James does not assume that sin always causes suffering, for he includes the particle 'if' (*kan*). Thus, although the exact link between personal sin and subsequent suffering differs from case to case, that there is a link is possible, though not always necessarily so.

The practices of private and public confession of sin were common in Judaism, being a significant part of the Day of Atonement, and confession of sin was recommended. The importance of confession was also taught amongst the early Christians; indeed, the tense of the verb (present imperative) in 5:16 suggests that it was expected that confession should form a regular part of the life of the community.

Although a number of interpretations may be offered for this passage, the one which fits the context most appropriately is that James is promising that confession of sin that has caused the suffering concerned should result in the restoration taking place. Although the text is not explicit, it seems obvious that any sins to be confessed are those committed by the perpetrators themselves. If they are confessed, and forgiveness granted, the prayers offered will be assumed to effect the healing process, if the sin was the reason for the suffering concerned. The remission of such sins presupposes a state of repentance and it is to this subject that James refers next in verse 16.

Stephen was a talented musician who regularly played in his local church with others as they led the congregation in worship every week. He began to experience a pain in his hands that made it very difficult to play his instrument and so he consulted his doctor, who was not able to diagnose a cause for the symptom. However, it did not ease, and in time he found it impossible to continue in the worship group. As a result, he approached the leaders in order that they might pray for him. During prayer, one of the leaders felt God suggest that Stephen may have been experiencing this pain in order that God could point out an area in his life that needed to be renounced. Speaking to Stephen on his own, he sensitively explored this with him, and Stephen confessed a moral failure of which he repented. A few hours after the confession and prayer with the leader, Stephen's pain miraculously disappeared. The sickness had been God's way of drawing Stephen's attention to the bigger problem that he needed to deal with and when that had been resolved the sickness was removed automatically. Not all sicknesses are caused by personal sin; indeed, most are not. However, on this occasion, Stephen had benefited from the painful but gracious and ultimately beneficial hand of God on his life, resulting in his adopting a more authentic Christian lifestyle and worshipping God more intimately, recognizing that God wanted to refine him so much that he chose to work in him individually through pain.

Application
- For practical application of this issue in a contemporary church setting, care is needed. It should not be assumed that sickness/suffering is always or even frequently caused by sin.

- However, if prayer is being offered for illness, the one offering the prayer should be aware of the possibility that sin may have resulted in the illness. Furthermore, wisdom should be sought from God and the person concerned to determine the validity of such a potential connection.

- If it has been determined that illness has been the consequence of sinful behaviour, lifestyle or actions, any confession should be offered in the presence of those who have been clearly harmed by it and/or in the presence of the leaders of that community, rather than in a wider context.

- It may be assumed that if sin was the cause of illness, once repentance has been effected, the person should expect to be restored physically.

Why does James include a story about Elijah, especially as it does not relate to healing?

Although it is clear from the rest of the letter of James that the author was well acquainted with the OT, the choice of Elijah in this context seems unusual. In a context of prayer for suffering believers, he chooses an incident from Elijah's life that refers to prayer for events in nature and not for healing. However, a number of important issues outlined in 5:14–16 receive confirmation in the Elijah narrative and so it acts as a helpful summarizing conclusion.

The value of fervent prayer

James describes the action of Elijah as 'fervent prayer' (5:17). The form of Greek used here reflects the Hebrew infinitive absolute, a popular tense indicating continuity or emphasis. Such a feature is associated with Jewish prayer and Elijah in particular (1 Kgs. 17:21, 18:43,44). James informs his readers that when they pray, they are to do it wholeheartedly.

The relationship between righteousness and prayer

Throughout his letter, James has demonstrated the value of a righteous lifestyle in relationship to prayer. Now, he reaffirms this relationship. Not only is Elijah revealed as a man of prayer in the OT, he is also depicted as a righteous person, being described as zealous for God (1 Kgs. 18:40, 19:14). It is because of his strong relationship with God that Elijah stands against powerful people (1 Kgs. 17:1, 18:21,30), readily obeys God (1 Kgs. 17:2–5,9,10, 18:1,2) and honestly presents himself to God (1 Kgs. 19:10). Miracles were performed by Elijah (1 Kgs. 17:8–24; 2 Kgs. 2:8). He was a man endued with the power to install kings (1 Kgs. 19:15,16), to prophesy their downfall (2 Kgs. 1:3,4) and to appoint prophets (1 Kgs. 19:16). Thus, James incorporates Elijah to encourage his readers to recognize the power available through prayer and the necessity of a righteous lifestyle to experience it.

The potential in prayer

It is possible that the inclusion of such an exalted figure may have led to discouragement on the part of the readership because of the honoured status of Elijah. Consequently, James explains that Elijah was similar to them. That which needs to be clarified is the particular aspect of similarity between Elijah and the readers. That James may be reminding his readers that they share a similar humanity with Elijah is a possibility. However, it is more likely that James is specifically drawing a comparison between Elijah and the readers with regard to suffering. In support of this, it may be argued that the OT portrays the suffering of Elijah in his discouragement (1 Kgs. 19:14), his fear (1 Kgs. 19:3) and the opposition towards him (1 Kgs. 18:17, 19:2). Coupled with this was the belief that Elijah would precede the coming of the Messiah and in that role would suffer (Mk. 9:12,13). That the illustration itself is located originally in a context of opposition where Elijah stood alone would help the readers identify with him in their sufferings. Elijah, who also suffered, experienced great results from his prayers. The potential is presented as being available for them also.

Suffering results from sin

James has already established the potential connection between sin and suffering and his inclusion of the illustration from the life of Elijah provides him with an opportunity to emphasize it. The incident in the life of

Elijah related to the idolatry of the people, as a result of which they suffered a drought. It was when they confessed their sin and renounced their allegiance to Baal (1 Kgs. 18:39) that rain was provided. Having established the possible connection between sin and suffering in 5:15, and having introduced the element of confession which results in restoration (5:16), James now provides an example of both features in the illustration drawn from the life of Elijah.

The significance of the will of God in prayer
In the Elijah narrative, James reminds his readers of the importance of praying in the will of God. He describes God's response, in the provision of drought and then rain, as being subsequent to prayer. However, in 1 Kings 17:1, the provision of the drought by God follows Elijah's prophecy. Similarly, although 1 Kings 18:42 implies that Elijah prayed for the rain, it is not certain, and James presents the action of God more clearly in the context of prayer than does the OT record. However, whatever action Elijah undertook, and he may have taken both, the determining factor was that he responded to a preceding and initiatory word of God, both with regard to the drought (Sirach 48:3) and the rain (1 Kgs. 18:1).

James offers the Elijah episode in a context of prayer, not prophecy, which appears to indicate a change in the course of the story. However, he anticipates the prayer being prompted by God in a similar way to prophecy; thus, the change in the presentation of the account is not as fundamental as it might initially appear, for whether by prayer or prophecy, Elijah has been seen to act in response to God. Both prayer and prophecy are secondary and, in this context, equivalent in value: the will of God is primary.

The prayer/prophecy preceded the response from God, but it was God who initiated them. The significance of the prayer/prophecy lies in the fact that they effected the will of God. Thus, James presents no distinction in principle between his record and that of 1 Kings, only a difference in methodology and presentation; the lesson remains constant in both. The determining factor for a positive response by God to prayer or prophecy is whether they were prompted by God.

Implications for the Contemporary Church

- James provides the church with guidelines for a unique opportunity to impart spiritual ministry, offering a comprehensive range of beneficial results to all believers who may be suffering from various problems. Consequently, not only does he use a number of different terms to describe the sufferings concerned, but he also describes the restoration to accommodate a wide range of healing processes depending on the particular need. He offers a path to wholeness and healing in their fullest sense. It is his conviction that, through prayer, support and restoration may be experienced by those in need.

- It is the responsibility of the members of the church to avail themselves of the opportunity to provide such support to those members of their community who are suffering. This will necessitate actively righteous lifestyles combined with compassion for others, and the wisdom and love to minister appropriately. In James's guidelines are located important characteristics that should be implemented in association with prayer.

- This advice, set in Jewish terms, needs to be re-contextualized for believers today so that they also can minister in the ways anticipated by James for his Christian constituency.

- Recognizing James as having provided a model, especially in so far as he anticipated an association with the will of God, is pastorally and theologically foundational.

- As such, it provides a useful complement to the Pauline expectation of charismatic gifts of healing.

7. The Role of the Spirit in Suffering

For much of Western Christianity, the experience of persecution is an infrequent one. At the same time, because of the wide availability of medical facilities, Western believers are less used to physical suffering than many others. Both facts have resulted in only a limited development of a theology of suffering by many. However, it has been a quest for some believers to determine a rationale for suffering and although the NT does not comprehensively explore this it does portray the Spirit as having central role in the life of the believer. An insight into the role of the Spirit in scenarios of suffering is important in order to appreciate better how believers can live fruitful lives despite some unfavourable contexts.

Suffering and the Spirit in Judaism

The Jews identified a number of reasons for suffering, including:

- Chastisement due to sin, resulting in sickness, plague, poverty, famine, drought and oppression (Lev. 26:16).

- Persecution (Jer. 20:2). It was the normative experience of prophets and other of God's servants.

- A desire by God to evaluate and improve his people (Jer. 29:10–13). As a result of testing through suffering, God was viewed as shaping his people for tasks he wished them to fulfil, their expected response being to be faithful and to persevere. Suffering was viewed as an opportunity of demonstrating commitment to God, as a result of which one was drawn closer to God.

- Satanic/demonic activity, though this was always under the sovereign rule of God (Job 2:4–7).

Suffering was explained largely as being beneficial in that persecution for the Jews' faith provided an opportunity for them to demonstrate their love for God. When it was the result of sin on their part, it helped to strengthen their resolve to fight against sin. It also acted as proof of their being God's people. Finally, suffering provided evidence of God's affection for them; thus, he disciplined them when they sinned and used suffering in his refining of their characters, thus enhancing their potential, because he loved them.

The Jews also identified a number of characteristics that resulted in appropriate responses to suffering. They believed that:

- They were living in the end times, a period associated with suffering (Dan. 8:23).

- God would vindicate them and deliver them from their suffering. (Ps. 35:24; Is. 50:8,9). Thus, it was appropriate to persist and be patient. The fact that Messiah was to come was viewed as evidence that the cries of the poor had been heard.

- God used suffering for his purposes (Gen. 50:20). Thus, the deaths of the martyrs were understood to have brought about the religio-political changes in the history of Israel.

- Suffering had vicarious value. The idea that suffering could atone for the sins of others is located in the writings of the Maccabees in the context of an exploration of reasons for martyrdom.

- Suffering provided opportunities to demonstrate care for others who were suffering. Thus, the prophets encouraged people to demonstrate their concern for those suffering either by helping to alleviate the suffering in a practical way, or by prayer, the suffering being the catalyst for that process.

- Suffering was always to be viewed in the context of a future hope (Mic. 4:4). Present suffering was to be explored in the knowledge that a better life was coming, when there would be no more sorrow.

- Some suffering was senseless due to one being a member of humanity where suffering is often indiscriminate (Ecc. 7:15) and is the result of living in a world which is associated with struggle and effort, the suffering identified as a mystery understood only by God.

In the OT, the Spirit empowered people to undertake extraordinary responsibilities that resulted in people being sustained in or redeemed from severe circumstances (Judg. 6:34, 11:29). On other occasions, the Spirit is described as being present in times of suffering (Ps. 51:11, 139:7), strengthening people in times of suffering (Is. 11:1–4), identifying some suffering as being caused by sin (Is. 48:16; Zech. 7:12) and offering hope after the suffering (Is. 43:19; Ezek. 37:11–14). In particular, the Messiah was expected to be the Spirit-endowed person who would support those who were suffering (Is. 42:1–5, 61:1–3).

Suffering and the Spirit in the Synoptics

The NT offers an innovative and distinct contribution to a better appreciation of the work of the Spirit in relationship to suffering. It is in the writings of Luke and Paul that the Spirit becomes a central element in this regard, though he is also introduced in the Synoptics with regard to suffering. For example, in situations where they may have felt isolated, Matthew (10:20; Mk. 13:11; Lk. 12:12) informed his readers that the Spirit was with them, inspiring them and empowering them. Their position of potential helplessness in the face of opposition forces was to be re-categorized as one of supreme sufficiency because of the presence of the Spirit. Although their families may have betrayed them, the Spirit would buttress them. Although their neighbours may slander them, the Spirit would support them.

The readers of each Synoptic Gospel would have benefited from the encouraging words of the writers as they affirmed the role of the Spirit to guide them in their responses to their accusers. Matthew's Jewish audience knew what it was like to be accused of betraying the ancient Jewish faith and to be marginalized by their religious constituencies. Mark's audience in Rome faced different pressures. To believe that Jesus was God was viewed as an act of folly, given that Jesus died and on a cross as a criminal. It was at Rome that the first significant persecutions were to take place and these would be of a different ferocity from those experienced elsewhere in the Empire up until that time. If ever there were believers who needed the comfort of a supernatural being who would give them the words to say and authority with which to present them, it was the readers of Mark's Gospel.

Luke's audience, including sophisticated Gentiles, would face yet another form of interrogation from those in their communities who would find the message of Jesus unacceptable when compared with the philosophies of the day. Christianity was intellectually unsatisfying and simplistic. Thus, he offers the promise that the Spirit will be with them, not just to provide words of support and defence for their beliefs but also to enable them to hold on to the truth and not to reject it in the face of opposition.

Suffering and the Spirit in Luke–Acts

Although Luke describes the Spirit inspiring prophecy and preaching, he also records his association with suffering. Thus, Simeon (2:25–35), described in association with the Spirit three times in three verses, prophesied of suffering for Mary and opposition for Jesus. The first recorded reference to Jesus (4:14–29) after his being baptized was at Nazareth, where he preached from Isaiah 61:1,2. Luke informs the readers (4:14) that Jesus was 'in the power of the Spirit', but the response of the people was not favourable, for they questioned him (4:22) and attempted to kill him (4:28,29). This opposition continued through the life of Jesus despite the fact that he ministered in association with the Spirit. In his second volume, Luke traces the same consequence of Spirit-inspired ministry receiving acceptance and also opposition in the lives of the Apostles.

Stephen functions as an example of a believer who was led by the Spirit (Acts 6:5,10, 7:55). Although there is a passing reference to the fact that he achieved signs and wonders (6:8), the immediate aftermath to the reference to Stephen's appointment as one of the Seven is that he also experienced opposition followed by his sermon and martyrdom. Although the Spirit is associated with his appointment, his miracles and his sermon, it is the opposition and suffering of the Spirit-inspired Stephen that Luke concentrates on (6:9 – 7:60). What is more remarkable is that Luke presents Stephen in parallel to Jesus. As Jesus was led by the Spirit and died a martyr's death, so also does Stephen. The message to the readers is clear. To be led by the Spirit assumes the possibility, indeed probability, of suffering.

Although the message of Acts is that the Gospel triumphs, it is in association with the fact that it does so through suffering. More particularly, the Spirit who sets the agenda for the development of the church and assures that it will succeed does so on a route often catalogued by opposition and suffering.

Suffering and the Spirit in Paul

In his letters, Paul comments less on healing than he does on suffering. That is not to say that healings ceased to occur. However, it is of significance to note that he writes more about suffering than he does about its removal. Instead, he speaks about its presence in the life of a believer as being normative, a point echoed elsewhere in the NT. Paul redeems the concept of suffering and centralizes it as a feature appropriate to all believers who experience it when they engage in doing the will of God. Thus, the young church in Thessalonica is affirmed by

Paul in that its members received the gospel with joy despite their great suffering, that experience resulting in their being imitated by many other believers (1 Thes. 1:6). Paul's concept of power can best be understood in the context of weakness and the latter is most clearly articulated in the experience of suffering. The Corinthians assumed that weakness and power were mutually exclusive; Paul sought to protect a corrective to this fallacy (2 Cor. 1:26, 13:9) and demonstrated that his sufferings, identified as hardships experienced in his apostolic ministry (2 Cor. 12:10), were divinely endorsed (12:9).

For Paul, weakness was understood as a prerequisite element in his life, necessary to identify the power of Christ. It is the vehicle through which the gospel was often revealed in his experience as it had been in the life of Christ. The implication of the promise from God to Paul, 'My grace is sufficient for you, for my power is made perfect in weakness,' is that it is also available for all other believers. For Paul, suffering had potential value. Although it is not to be assumed that all suffering is good, it is to be maintained that, on occasions, it may be harnessed by God for the benefit of the believer and the development of the Kingdom.

Paul wrote his letters against a background of social, financial, verbal and physical suffering. The context of the readers may be easily overlaid in our contemporary world in which Christians are suffering. The world is as alien a home for many contemporary believers as it was in the early years of the church.

Paul removes the concept of suffering from the assumption that it is associated with the displeasure of God. Instead, he associates suffering with positive benefits. Thus, whereas the Galatians assumed that weakness in a representative of a god indicated an insignificant deity, Paul presents his suffering as the divinely ordained plan of God as a result of which the Galatians heard the good news of Jesus (Gal. 4:14). Similarly, the thorn in the flesh (2 Cor. 12:7–10) is presented as of benefit to Paul in that its objective was to remind Paul of his own weakness and inability to succeed without the support of God. However, as well as commenting a great deal on suffering, that which he offers as an extra dimension with regard to suffering is the role of the Spirit to support the suffering believer.

The Spirit is associated with and works through suffering

The consequence of being a child of God is that one will suffer (Rom. 8:17). However, in that suffering, the power of God is made manifest. The weakness of the believer referred to in Romans 8:26 results in the unilateral involvement of the Spirit to support the believer in his or her time of powerlessness. His role is to empower believers, especially those who are suffering. Although the identification of that weakness is not clarified, the term used by Paul is interpreted variously elsewhere as sickness, weariness, weakness (of many kinds) and various forms of suffering. That which is not disputed is that the role of the Spirit is to support those who are suffering.

The Spirit is not only related to miracles, signs and wonders but also suffering and weakness. It is not the case that life lived in the shadow of the cross and life lived in the power of the Spirit are mutually exclusive. There is no contrast to be drawn between a theology of the cross and a theology of the Spirit. The former does not signify suffering and the latter glory. Both are complementary, involving suffering and glory; indeed, glory through suffering. Thus, when Paul describes his life of suffering in 2 Corinthians 2:14–16 that was associated with his ministry, which resulted in their hearing the Gospel, he concludes that the Spirit of God has been part of the enterprise (3:3). Similarly, he associates suffering with being led by the Spirit (Acts 14:22). Luke writes with a similar agenda, identifying Paul's journey to Jerusalem to suffer not only as being prophesied by the Spirit (21:11) but also resulting from the leading of the Spirit (Acts 20:22).

The Spirit provides adoption for believers

The issue of suffering as a believer in Romans 8 is located in the context of adoption. Paul has been declaring the difference made by the presence of the Spirit in the lives of believers (Rom. 8:1–13). Now, he declares the activity of the Spirit that results in believers being identified as the children of God while the world in which they live and circumstances of life abandon them to suffering. This relationship as adopted children of God is certain because the Spirit who is part of their lives is none other than the Spirit of adoption who, coming into their presence, places them in God's presence. The reference to the cry of 'Abba! Father' may relate to a joyful consideration of their relationship with God or their cry in time of need. Whatever the occasion, the Spirit acts as a reliable friend who affirms that such a relationship is valid and not presumptuous.

Paul is not declaring that believers must suffer in order to receive their adoption. Rather, he is reflecting on the fact that the readers may well suffer physically and as a result of their faith (the persecution of Christians by Nero [AD 64] is only a few years off), but they do so in association with their Saviour. This earthly existence is only the preface to a life characterized by glory. Present sufferings, whatever their identity, do not undermine the believers' right to be called children of God, such a position being determined by God, assured by the Spirit, to be enjoyed eternally.

The Spirit seals the believer

The introductory verses of 2 Corinthians catalogue Paul's sufferings (1:5) on the Corinthians' behalf (1:6) and identify their partnership with him in suffering (1:7). He graphically describes the intensity of his past afflictions (1:8ff.) and informs them of his reliance on their prayers for him (1:10). In a context of suffering, he reminds them of the role of the Spirit to seal believers (1:22). Although not specifically mentioned, the reference to sealing most likely refers to that which takes place at salvation.

The concept of 'sealing with the Spirit' provides Paul with an opportunity to explore the radical nature of the supportive role of the Spirit to the believers in their sufferings. The practice of sealing letters, objects and even people was common in the ancient world. The seal represented a number of features, each of which help explicate the comprehensive nature of the Spirit's involvement in the life of a believer.

Fundamentally, the seal signified ownership; that which was sealed was owned by someone. The fact that believers are sealed with the Spirit indicates that the one who arranged for the sealing to occur, namely Christ, owns them. In a society that was quickly becoming inhospitable to Christians, it was of considerable encouragement to them to realize that someone had chosen to own them and had affirmed this by the presence of none other than the Spirit in them. While physical sickness and/or suffering may have resulted in their marginalization, the Spirit is defined as centralizing them in a family framework in which God functions as their father.

Secondly, the seal signified security. In the commercial centre of Corinth, buyers would seal goods that they intended to purchase by stamping them with a seal. It indicated that the goods were spoken for; they were no longer for sale. The Spirit is described as similarly functioning as security for believers. Not only does someone own them; he also happens to be the one who owns all authority. To seek to harm a believer would thus be equivalent to attempting to harm God.

Finally, the seal signifies that the object sealed is valuable. To a group of Christians who will soon experience persecution, when they will be treated as worthless objects, Paul reminds them that they are valuable to God. Although marginalized by society, the Spirit has sealed them. As members of an ancient society, they were used to physical diseases, many of which were incurable, and with all the attendant disadvantages, pain and frustration they brought. Paul's message is clear – the Spirit is their envelope of security in which they live with God, his grace being available for their particular needs.

The Spirit acts as a guarantee

In Ephesians 1:14 Paul uses the word *arrabōn* (also 2 Cor. 1:21,22, 5:5); each reference has reference to the Spirit. This is a technical term for a first installment or guarantee. The Spirit is God's downpayment in the believer's life and, as such, he acts as a guarantee and a taste of the future. Two things in particular are guaranteed: (i) believers will possess the inheritance graciously promised by God to them; (ii) God will possess the inheritance chosen by himself, the church, for himself. The cumulative effect is to provide the readers with a sense of well-being and security; they are secure beyond their understanding and the Spirit is their guarantee.

There was a great deal of uncertainty in the ancient world. In Ephesus, a fire was kept burning to act as a guarantee that the city would not be destroyed. On a broader level, security was an important feature of Ephesian life, represented by a six-mile-long wall around the city. Life for the people of the time was fragile. Issues of health were frequently on their minds, though for the vast majority it was not an area over which they had much control. However, if health issues dominated much of the thoughts of people, life after death was much more uncertain for Jews and Gentiles alike. Paul, however, is convinced of his eternal destiny and encourages his readers to be as confident about theirs, concluding with the fact that the presence of the Spirit in their lives acts as a constant reminder of their eternal security despite their present struggles.

The Spirit inspires hope

Paul ascribes a significant role to the Spirit with regard to the concept of hope (Rom. 5:3–5). When the pressure of one's situation results in despair edging ever closer, Paul describes the presence of the Spirit as enabling believers to retain the belief that their suffering is the prelude to something better. His promise to them is that this suffering is to be considered in the light of the fact that as the children of God they will be glorified with him hereafter (8:17). The Spirit enables the suffering believer to abound in hope (15:13), the word 'abound' meaning abundance, to the point of excess. Paul thus encourages his readers to believe that their sufferings are not resulting from the superior power of the enemies of God. On the contrary, God is supreme and the Spirit affirms this fact (8:28) and the glory of the future will wipe out the contradictions of the present.

The Spirit inspires love

The first time love is mentioned in Romans (5:5) is in the context of suffering (5:3,4) and the Spirit. The Spirit has an important part to play in channeling the love of God to believers with lavish generosity. Paul expresses the notion of the love of God in an experiential more than an intellectual way. The reference to love being located in the believers' hearts further expresses the emotional nature of this reception of God's love. Paul expects God's love for the believer to be felt. The tense of the verb, 'has been poured', is perfect; in Greek, this has the meaning of an act in the past that has ongoing significance. The experience of the love of God is thus intended to be an ongoing reality for the believer, having been imparted at salvation, but especially present in times of suffering.

The presence of suffering should therefore not be assumed to indicate the absence of God. On the contrary, given the fact that God is best represented by his central characteristic of love, his guaranteed presence with believers indicates that they are the direct recipients of that love. All suffering needs to be considered in the context of the eternal love of God for those who are suffering.

The Spirit helps believers

The Spirit is being described as doing something *for* believers. In the context of the weakness of believers, the Spirit is presented as operating on their behalf (Rom. 8:26).

Paul uses a rare verb for 'help' in the Bible and prefaces it with another word (*huper*) that emphasizes the intensity of the help offered. Not only does the Spirit help, but also he significantly helps those who are weak and suffering as a consequence. Paul is painting a picture with words to explore the fact that the Spirit in us is in partnership with the Father to support us in all our situations, not just when life is at its lowest, but throughout all our days; when nightmares control our next steps; through the storms when all we can taste is our tears; in the hurricane when we hunt for a haven; but also when we can see a golden horizon, when dreams come true and life is too wonderful for words. God isn't there just when we need him; he's also there when we don't.

The word used by Paul to describe the way the Spirit helps us is rare and includes the concept of support or partnership. He doesn't just help us but does so from a position of being with us, alongside us, in our shoes; not just once but continually and continuously. This is not support from a distance, not help from another world, but closer than a whisper. The word used by Paul for 'help' is associated with another occasion where it is used, namely Luke 10:40, where Martha asks for Mary to help her. She is asking that Mary will hold her hand in the helping process. God is so close that he can take our hand and charge us with his energy.

The Spirit prays for believers

Paul refers to the fact that the Spirit prays for believers in their weakness (Rom. 8:26,27). Paul's reference to the Spirit praying is a metaphor which must be carefully unwrapped. He is declaring a truth that is precious and therefore to be appropriated, but also a mystery and therefore not necessarily to be completely understood, though to be explored intellectually and experientially. The picture is of the Spirit, who is God, so intimately relating to believers that for a moment it is as if his closeness to them is greater than it is to God, enabling him to pray for them.

This concept of the Spirit demonstrating this quality of empathy with believers is remarkable. The believer is not praying; the Spirit is praying for the believer. This does not mean that Christians are inactive. However, for the believers, the fact that they do not know how to pray is part of their weakness. Nevertheless, they are encouraged to recognize that the Spirit who affirms them (Rom. 8:16,17) himself prays for them (8:26) in accordance with God's will (8:27) and purpose (8:28). The Spirit is speaking out loud for our benefit so we can hear his heartbeat for us.

The Spirit groans with believers

Paul refers to the fact that the Spirit identifies with believers with groans that are too deep for words (Rom. 8:26). The term translated 'too deep for words' is of significance. It may be translated 'without words' or 'unable to be expressed'. Paul may therefore be not seeking to identify the occurrence of the Spirit's intercession on the behalf of the believer but simply to specify that he is doing so and that the believer may depend on the fact that such intercession is full of sincerity and meaning, even though he or she may not hear it. It may be silent but it taps at the very heart of the fact that the Spirit is committed to suffering believers and expresses the most complete advocacy on behalf of the believer. The significance of the Spirit being involved on the part of the believer is that he will ensure that God's will be enacted. This is a foregone conclusion, since he is God.

The Spirit offers a new perspective on suffering

Thus, believers are informed that the suffering they experience is part of a wider context. Believers are not exempt from the suffering experienced by the world; in reality, they participate in its pain (Rom. 8:18–23), but so does the Spirit. The suffering experienced by both is not the fault of the sufferers; rather, it is sin that is at fault and both creation and the church suffer as a result. However, both will be redeemed from this situation when God resolves the issue of sin, while the expectation of Paul is that the Spirit-empowered church should positively impact the suffering world while also being individually and corporately supported by the Spirit.

Implications for the Contemporary Church

- At first sight, it may be assumed that a basic aspect of the ministry of Jesus was to remove suffering. However, not all suffering was remedied by Jesus, nor is there evidence to suggest that this was the most important part of his agenda. In the ministry of Jesus, there is little reference to slavery, the oppression of the Roman Empire, the crippling poverty of the people caused by the taxation burden, or the many other aspects of the life of the Jews that called for a radical solution to establish justice. Indeed, rather than cause all suffering to flee with a flick of his fingers, he forecast suffering for his followers (Mk. 10:38–44).

  Similarly, although Jesus healed many people, few followed him and many rejected him; although Jesus functioned authoritatively, he himself suffered. The path of the Messiah was the path that commenced in the clothes of a baby in a manger and concluded in the nakedness of a cross and the burial clothes of a tomb. It will be surprising if the testimony of his followers is that they lived lives of luxury and limited suffering when their Lord and Master did not. The book of Acts and the lives of the Apostles demonstrate that his sufferings continued in their lives. As his mission was born and ended in suffering, so also the mission of the early church was conducted in the context of suffering.

The success of the mission of Jesus and the early church was not in spite of the suffering experienced but as a consequence of it; not because suffering is meritorious in its own right, but because it is the path chosen beforehand by the Spirit (Acts 9:16, 14:22) and therefore to be expected in times of growth and assumed to result in growth.

- The issue of suffering must not be overlooked by believers as God's way of refining believers. Although suffering is not to be experienced in heaven and is not intrinsically good, God nevertheless has the capacity to use it, on occasions, to serve his purposes on our behalf.

- Suffering must be viewed in the context of eternity, where all our questions may be answered in the knowledge that the God who directs our lives does so not callously and uncaringly, but authoritatively with love and compassion.

- It is also to be recognized that suffering is part of life in a fallen world that affects God's people as it has always done. However, at the same time, believers are part of God's family with responsibility for support and prayer for one another.

- Suffering should be viewed as a valid context for reflecting God and understood as a pathway of victory as much as a situation that is the result of healing or some other supernatural restoration.

- In a world that was and still is often dominated by suffering, it is instructive to note that the NT writers often identify the role of the Spirit in contexts of weakness and suffering. Although suffering is inextricably linked to life and Christians are not immune to it, it is to be remembered that it is an earthbound condition and the Spirit's involvement in the suffering of the believer is certain, motivated by love and comprehensive wisdom.

- The role of the Spirit in supporting believers when they suffer and enabling that suffering to benefit them and others is to be presented as a subject worthy of exploration. This will result in all concerned being able to realize the significant commitment of the Spirit to them in their individual circumstances, his aim being to enable all believers to achieve the destiny and potential set before them by God.

8. The Final Word

To use the Bible as a guidebook for understanding healing and suffering necessitates careful reading. Some of the information was specifically written for different audiences and particular purposes. The Gospels demonstrated Jesus' healings as evidence of his authority as the Saviour and Son of God, resulting in his authority to establish the Kingdom of God, forgive sins and provide people with the opportunity to develop relationships with God. The letters of James and Paul provide guidelines for healing praxis and a better appreciation of the significance of suffering for believers. Also, the role of the Spirit and the community of believers are integral components in the development of clear frameworks for healing and suffering in the lives of believers today. The following summary is a useful conclusion:

- The Old Testament presents God as a healer. This characteristic helps define him as God.

- The Gospels present Jesus as a healer. This helps define him as the Messiah and Saviour who came to initiate the Kingdom (rule) of God. Furthermore, the Gospels record the healings and exorcisms of Jesus to demonstrate the uniqueness of his person and mission.

- The Acts of the Apostles provides examples of the ongoing healing ministry in the early church, mainly through Peter and Paul. Furthermore, it presents Jesus as still healing, the Apostles and others functioning in healing in ways that are reminiscent of Jesus in his mission activity. The ascended Christ is still present in the church.

- The letters of Paul impart limited information about the charismatic and spontaneous nature of the gifts of the Spirit as they relate to healing. Paul reflects the interim period between the initiation and consummation of the Kingdom. Although healings still occur, suffering is also present and not all illness is removed. Nevertheless, on occasions, God still heals via the gifts of healings. When he chooses not to bring restoration, the promise of 2 Corinthians 12:9, 'My grace is sufficient for you, for my power is made perfect in weakness,' is a strong support.

- The letter of James provides guidelines for healing praxis to be undertaken by members of the local church on behalf of one another. James reflects the same premise that healings still occur and he provides guidelines for preparing for this possibility while giving advice concerning the role of the believers to minister to those suffering from varied forms of weakness. This advice, albeit set in Jewish terms, needs to be re-contextualized for the contemporary church so that it also can minister in the ways anticipated by James for his Christian constituency.

- 1 and 2 Peter, Hebrews and Revelation give particular advice to believers who are suffering persecution.

What are some of the Important Issues to Remember when Praying for those Suffering?

God is bigger than the problem

When we don't see God working as we think he should, we often get confused and worried. Our logic tells us God can do anything, and so when there's a problem that he doesn't solve or a prayer that he doesn't answer in the way we asked, or guidance that he doesn't clarify, we assume that we're to blame or the devil's too strong. Most of the time, nothing could be further from the truth. It's just that our conclusions as to how to resolve the situation are often not his. Similarly, there is no danger that the devil is stopping God doing what he wants to do. The devil is not a competitor to God nor is he a dark force that comes close to winning the war. He was always only a creation of God who thought he could replace God. At that moment, he became a defeated angel whose demise was affirmed by Jesus in his death and resurrection and whose destiny was determined by God before he was created.

We have questions; God has reasons

God has power, but he also has priorities, and sometimes the latter are different from ours. Our role is to trust God. Elisabeth Elliot is the wife of one of five young American missionaries who went to the Amazon jungle to share the Gospel for the first time with the Auca Indians. In the spring of 1956, Jim Elliott and his friends were killed by the people they had come to save. On January 11, 1956, Elisabeth Elliot wrote these words knowing that it was likely that her three young children would not see their father this side of heaven because the missionaries had not radioed their families for five days and two bodies had been seen floating in the water. 'I have no idea what I will do if Jim is dead, but the Lord knows and I am at rest. We hope for final word tomorrow and trust our loving Father who never wastes anything.' Later she wrote, 'God knows what he is doing and he is not under any obligation to make us any explanations.'[1]

God's power is for overcoming life's problems, not for escaping them

God's power is awesome, but it isn't always there to make the mountains melt, but to make them manageable; not always to make the desert disappear, the darkness depart or the fog fade away, but to keep us, care for us and carry us to through, enabling us to grow in the process. Against the forces of the evil foe, the finger of God is enough to keep us safe. When I think God has moved his finger from my life, I'm wrong. I may not know all the answers, but I am learning to trust the one who has set the agenda.

God loves us

God loved us before we were born, before our parents were born, before anyone was born. Before we had thought about God, God had already thought about us. Before we lifted our fingers to him, he had stretched his hands down to us. Before we had bowed the knee, he had already bent his ear; before we had expressed hope, he had left heaven; before we dared to say sorry, he had died to save us. Before we proceeded towards a relationship with God, God had already started the process. He led us

---

[1] R. T. Hitt, *Jungle Pilot* (London: Hodder & Stoughton, 1960), p. 297.

to himself; we who could not search for him; we who could not even accidentally bump into him. God is the God of the previous, who finishes before we start, who says hello to us when we're hiding from him.

In a world of easy promises and empty pledges it's natural to be sceptical about guarantees that seem too good to be true. And God's love and grace are two of those guarantees that can seem too good to be true. Paul tells the Corinthians about one of these guarantees that God has given him – 'My grace is sufficient for you' (2 Cor. 12:9). When our children were much younger, we went for walks in the country. On one of these treks, we crossed a stream that was too wide for their little legs. Although they had boundless energy, they lacked ability; they saw the other side but their focus was on the gap; it was easy for me, and because I carried them, it was easy for them. Similarly, God provides strength for our struggles, wisdom for our wilderness, love for our loneliness, friendship for our fear, forgiveness for our failure, hope for our heartache, joy for our journey and grace to reach our goals.

When you look at another mountain, tell yourself that when the mountain has been worn away by the winds of time, you'll still be alive; when the sun has cooled into a block of ice, you'll still be sparkling bright; when the rivers have all run dry, you'll still be bubbling with life because God has planned eternity with you in mind. In giving himself to us, he has changed us from what we were, and is committed to transforming us into what he wants us to be – like him, so that we will live our future in the fullness of his life. Our future is based on the fact that God is for us, unconditionally. That's grace. No satisfactory reason, no understandable explanation, but a marvellous mystery and an inexhaustible journey of discovery.

A wealthy English family were horrified one afternoon to hear that their young son, Winston Churchill, had nearly drowned in the swimming pool. He was saved by the gardener. Years later, that same child became the British Prime Minister and was stricken with pneumonia. The king called for the best doctor in England to ensure he recovered. The doctor was Alexander Fleming, the developer of penicillin and the son of the gardener who had saved him from drowning. Churchill had been saved by the father and the son. God's commitment to us, however, is threefold, for not only has the Father saved us through the sacrifice of the Son, but the Spirit guarantees to accompany us on our journey. God doesn't see us from afar but follows us with his eyes, hears our heartbeat, knows our name and stays with us when we stop.

Listen

Prayer is the activity of me responding to God as well as me speaking to God. Prayer is not always to be defined as an activity in which we first offer a request to God; it should also incorporate time spent waiting for God to speak to us. When my daughter was very young, I was driving to the airport with her to pick up my wife. 'Why doesn't God speak to me?' she said. I knew what she meant. As Christians, we talk about God speaking to us, but we have very limited notions as to how he does. Perhaps he will speak through a sermon, prophecy or personal Bible reading. Few of us expect an audible voice or an angelic visitation. But the fact is, he's everywhere, and I'm learning the importance of identifying where he is so that I can respond to him, whatever he says, however he says it. I remember reading of a book that offered many guidelines for getting God's attention. We don't need to learn how to get God's attention; he's already perfectly attentive to our situations.

When it comes to prayer for those who are suffering, my practice for many years has been based on the fact that God has given me two ears – one to listen to the person concerned and one to listen to God so that he can guide me in my prayer and my ministry. Finally, and most importantly, expect God to respond to your prayer. He may respond differently from that which we may have hoped for, but he will always respond positively to the believer who comes to him on behalf of another.

Selected Reading

Literature on Healing

Avalos, H., *Health Care and the Rise of Christianity* (Peabody: Hendrickson, 1999).

Brown, M. L., *Israel's Divine Healer* (Carlisle: Paternoster Press, 1995).

Farah, C., *From the Pinnacle of the Temple* (Plainfield: Logos, no date).

Dunn, R., *Will God Heal Me?* (Eastbourne: Kingsway, 1997).

Gee, D., *Trophimus, I Left Sick: Our Problem of Divine Healing* (Clapham: Elim, 1952).

Goldingay, J. (ed.), *Signs, Wonders and Healing* (Leicester: Inter-Varsity Press, 1989).

Gunstone, J., *The Lord is Our Healer* (London: Hodder & Stoughton, 1986).

Harper, M., *The Healings of Jesus* (London: Hodder & Stoughton, 1986).

Kydd, R. A. N., *Healing through the Centuries: Models for Understanding* (Peabody: Hendrickson, 1988).

MacNutt, F., *Healing* (Notre Dame: Ave Maria Press, 1974).

Pearson, M., *Christian Healing* (London: Hodder & Stoughton, 1996).

Thomas, J. C., *The Devil, Disease and Deliverance* (Sheffield: Sheffield Academic Press, 1998).

Twelftree, G., *Jesus the Miracle Worker* (Downers Grove: InterVarsity Press, 1999).

Warrington, K., 'Healing and Exorcism: the Path to Wholeness' in K. Warrington (ed.), *Pentecostal Perspectives* (Carlisle: Paternoster Press, 1998), pp. 147–75.

——, *Jesus the Healer: Paradigm or Unique Phenomenon* (Carlisle: Paternoster Press, 2000).

Wilkinson, J., *The Bible and Healing* (Edinburgh: Handsel Press, 1998).

Wimber, J. and Springer, K., *Power Healing* (London: Hodder & Stoughton, 1986).

Woolmer, J., *Healing and Deliverance* (London: Hodder & Stoughton, 1999).

Literature on Suffering

Brand, P. and Yancey, P., *Pain: The Gift Nobody Wants* (New York: HarperCollins, 1993).

Carson, D. A., *How Long, O Lord* (Leicester: IVP, 1990).

Dau, I. M., *Suffering and God* (Nairobi: Paulines, 2002).

Dunn, R., *When Heaven is Silent* (Waco: Word, 1994).

Elliot, E., *A Path through Suffering* (Carlisle: OM, 1997).

Farley, E., *Divine Empathy: A Theology of God* (Minneapolis: Fortress, 1996).

Fiddes, P., *The Creative Suffering of God* (Oxford: Clarendon, 1988).

Hall, D. J. *God and Human Suffering: An Exercise in the Theology of the Cross* (Minneapolis: Augsburg, 1986).

Hauerwas, S., *Naming the Silences: God, Medicine and the Problem of Suffering* (Grand Rapids: Eerdmans, 1990).

Kushner, H. S., *When Bad Things Happen to Good People* (New York: Avon, 1981).

McGrath, A. E., *Suffering and God* (Grand Rapids: Zondervan, 1995).

Richmond, K. D., *Preaching to Sufferers: God and the Problem of Pain* (Nashville: Abingdon, 1988).

Walters, G., *Why do Christians Find it so Hard to Grieve?* (Carlisle: Paternoster Press, 1997).

Yancey, P., *Where is God when it Hurts?* (London: Pickering & Inglis, 1998).

Index

Healing and Wholeness: Reflections on the Healing Ministry

Robert J. Hillman with Coral Chamberlain and Linda Harding

Presenting a biblical basis for the ministry of healing and emphasising the centrality of the gospel, Robert Hillman reflects on current views about healing, the Holy Spirit and the renewal of the church.

- Biblical 'holistic healing'
- Why are some not healed?
- Demons and demonisation – what does the Bible say?
- Unity and the healing of the church

Written for all Christians regardless of denominational, doctrinal or theological preferences, Robert Hillman provides practical guidelines and reflection on the healing ministry and the place of healing in today's church.

'Our postmodern world is hungry for teaching about spiritual healing, but Christians are often afraid to deal with this issue. This book will help answer their questions and overcome their reservations.'
Tony Campolo, Professor of Sociology, Eastern College, St Davids, PA.

'In this introductory overview, Robert Hillman makes a wise and compassionate contribution that will help churches of all shades make progress in their care for one another.'
Jonathan Lamb, Regional Secretary for Europe and the CIS International Fellowship of Evangelical Students.

1-870345-35-5

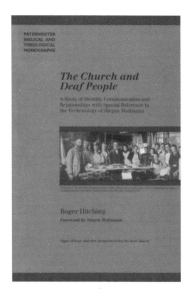

The Church and Deaf People: A Study of Identity, Communication and Relationships with Special Reference to the Ecclesiology of Jürgen Moltmann

Roger Hitching

The Church and Deaf People examines Jürgen Moltmann's ecclesiology from the specific perspective of deaf people, who form a minority group within our society and who have been marginalized and effectively oppressed.

Inspired by his contact with deaf people (after his first wife became profoundly deaf) and mindful of the example of his deaf grandmother, Roger Hitching sensitively examines the history and present experience of deaf people in relation to Moltmann's radical ecclesiology. This book confidently addresses the shortage of theological reflection on deaf people's experience of church and challenges us all to question 'the perspective of the dominant hearing culture.'

'I read this excellent work by Roger Hitching with growing fascination and felt enriched on every page. It opened up new theological perspectives of which previously I had been quite unaware.'
Jürgen Moltmann, Professor of Emeritus of Systematic Theology in the Protestant Faculty of the University of Tübingen

1-84227-222-5